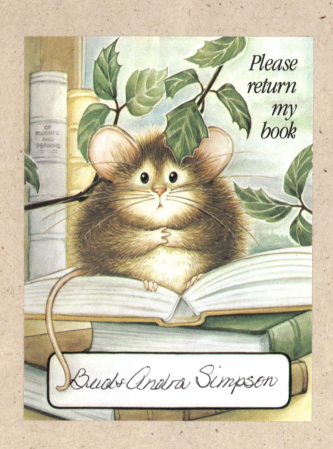

Please return my book

Bud & Andra Simpson

NO GREATER LOVE

NO GREATER LOVE

and Other True Stories of Courage and Conviction

KRIS MACKAY

Deseret Book Company
Salt Lake City, Utah

©1982 Deseret Book Company
All rights reserved
Printed in the United States of America

No part of this book may be reproduced in any
form or by any means without permission in writing
from the publisher, Deseret Book Company,
P.O. Box 30178, Salt Lake City, Utah 84130

First printing March 1982
Second printing July 1982
Third printing April 1984
Fourth printing March 1985

Library of Congress Cataloging in Publication Data

Mackay, Kris.
    No greater love, and other true stories of courage
and conviction.

    1. Church of Jesus Christ of Latter-day Saints—
Biography. I. Title.
BX8693.M32   289.3′3 [B]   81-22123
ISBN 0-87747-906-2   AACR2

*To those special people whose
experiences made this book possible,
with my gratitude and love*

Contents

NO GREATER LOVE

and Other True Stories of Courage and Conviction

1

No
Greater
Love

"How much do you love the people you serve?"

This thought-provoking question was directed to Elder Richard Blodgett as he sat with elbows resting lightly on a table in the home of Brother and Sister Krebs in Wuppertal, Germany. It was a question in answer to *his* question, actually.

Once a month this good brother and sister invited all twelve zone missionaries into their home for dinner—no small undertaking at best. Today was Thanksgiving, and they'd gone all out in a country that doesn't even celebrate Thanksgiving.

Two discarded doors were positioned on sawhorses and pushed together. Their best cloth of white linen with an intricate lace border covered the double surface and transformed the doors into one elegant table long enough to seat fourteen. It looked inviting with the candle and flower centerpiece, even though, as usual, half of the table was laid with dishes of one pattern while the other half held plates from a different set.

Twelve healthy missionaries consume enormous amounts of food, as anyone experienced in feeding missionaries will agree, and the Krebs family wasn't all that well-to-do. Entertaining on this scale had to be a hardship for them. Not that the elders ever complained. Partaking of Sister Krebs's home-cooked meals was the month's culinary highlight for the lucky guests, most of whom had neither time nor talent for concocting anything fancy on their own.

Rick sat at one end of the long table with his host. Dinner was finished now, but they still sat contentedly around remains of the feast. Chairs were pushed comfortably back, and relaxed diners separated into spontaneous conversational groups.

Rick pulled colored balloons from a jacket pocket, blew them up, and began to form them into animal figures such as clowns make at circuses. He used this handy trick to protect himself during casual conversations. He was new to the mission field and not yet proficient in the language. Working with balloons furnished a few seconds to sort over a phrase or two he didn't immediately grasp.

He finished the first figure and handed it to the man at his right to be identified. This was harder than it sounds, for Brother Krebs is blind. Fingertips probed over rounded curves and jutting angles, and several figures were identified correctly. When he called out "Elephant," Rick quickly seized the mouse's nose, pulled, and laughed. *"Ja, ja, Brudder, das ist ein Elephant."*

The thing that puzzled Rick was why this good man and his petite wife went to so much trouble and expense. A warm meal for a pair of young men far from home was understandable. But monthly feasts for the entire complement of the zone? He asked about it. Instead of the expected answer, he was hit with that strange question: "How much do you love the people you serve?"

Rick considered it seriously. He believed he *did* love this people among whom he labored. He knew he'd grown very fond of them. He admired and respected the German population at large for the way they'd come out of two world wars with national pride intact, and for the enormous suffering he knew they'd endured. The man posing this enigmatic question was certainly no stranger to pain or suffering. He was scarred and blinded by one of the war's incendiary bombs, and yet he, his wife and five children, grown now and on their own, continued year after year as stalwarts in the faith.

Silence fell between the two men. Both were lost in thought. At last Brother Krebs spoke. "Let me tell you a story," he said softly.

*   *   *   *   *

It was wartime. American missionaries had been pulled out of the country and went home to be drafted. Some of them returned, but this time they came as sworn enemies.

One former elder wasn't happy with the situation. A corporal with a reconnaissance group, he went out with small advance patrols to set up routes of attack. Streets of the towns were familiar to him; he'd tracted them out such a short while ago.

He was unhappy for another reason. He felt out of place among his comrades. The sergeant, particularly, was a new breed to him—burly, swaggering, contemptuous of signs of weakness in the men beneath him. And this boy who neither drank, smoked, nor caroused was definitely a thorn in the sergeant's side, a youth he felt personally committed to boost into manhood. The air between them was charged, just waiting for a showdown. The corporal bit his lip and reminded himself he owed allegiance to the uniform, if not to the man himself.

Using great restraint, he got by without direct confrontation until the afternoon he watched a group of German citizens being rounded up for looting in a town the Allies had just taken over. There were strict rules against looting, but when people were starving, rules were hard to enforce.

The sergeant manhandled the group roughly. Suddenly, without thinking of the consequences, the corporal acted on impulse. He brushed his superior aside and with obvious joy and cries of recognition, threw his arms protectively around one aging gentleman.

The sergeant was furious. He grabbed the corporal's arm, yanked him aside, and growled angrily, "What do you think you're doing?"

"Sergeant, I don't expect you to understand, but I love this man. I was a missionary before the war, and I taught him the gospel. He was the only person I ever baptized. He's a good man!"

If the sergeant was furious before, he turned a livid purple now. To have his authority challenged in front of the other men was intolerable.

"Insubordination, corporal?" he said with eyes narrowed. "This man was caught looting, and apparently you need a lesson in loyalty. Okay. Early tomorrow morning he will be shot—and you'll be doing the shooting!"

The young man's face turned chalky white but he didn't flinch. "No! I won't do it, sarge," he said. "There's no way you can make me do it."

That did it. Regaining authority was the only thing important now. "Let me understand you, corporal. Are you disobeying a direct command in time of war? If so, it's my duty to remind you that that's an offense punishable by death. We're moving fast, and I'm the law out here. We don't have time for a courtmartial. You have until morning to make up your mind. At five in the morning that looter will be staring down the muzzles of a firing squad. You'll either be on the business end of a rifle, or you'll be standing beside your friend. Take your choice."

* * * * *

Brother Krebs paused in his narrative. Other conversations around the table had long since trickled to a halt as one by one the dinner guests tuned in to the gripping story. He couldn't see the wide eyes turned in his direction, but he sensed how deeply they were moved.

Silently each missionary questioned himself: what would I do if caught in this same life-threatening trap? They'd been called to spread the gospel of love. Did they truly understand the meaning of the word? "Greater love hath no man than this, that a man lay down his life for his friends." (John 15:13.)

Brother Krebs sighed. He shifted his weight in the chair; then in a trembling voice he continued.

"The frightened corporal bravely stood his ground. The next morning he and his elderly German brother stood side by side and were shot down together in a lonely field not far from here.

"You ask me why I go out of my way to show affection for American missionaries? Brethren, that man was my father."

2

The Nine-Ingredient Pie

Life in Ferron, Emery County, Utah, hadn't been easy for Gwendolyn Killpack. She was small for her age and somewhat frail. Her mother had died before they had time to really know each other, and Gwen had no memory of her at all. Her mother's sister moved into the home to care for the family, and in due time she became Gwen's stepmother.

Gwen truly loved her new mother. She called her Aunt Emma, but in every important sense they were mother and daughter, perhaps closer in spirit than most "flesh of my flesh."

Brother Killpack was a well-known member of the community. He taught school besides having various church, business, and political interests. Important visitors stayed in the Killpack home and required frequent entertaining.

Gwen helped out willingly. Once when she was seven, she memorized a little speech of welcome for the governor's overnight visit.

Then Aunt Emma was stricken with serious illness and became a semi-invalid. Gwen helped out more than ever. She didn't mind staying close to home at an age when most little girls keep house only for dolls. She performed many simple tasks under her stepmother's direction. There were all kinds of things a little girl could do to be of help.

One afternoon Aunt Emma called Gwen to her bedside. With her arms around the little girl and tears in her eyes, she expressed her appreciation for the countless times Gwen had put aside her own pleasures in order to keep the house running smoothly, and her gratitude for the love they shared. Then Gwen's beloved second mother died.

Gwen was barely thirteen when full responsibility for the big farmhouse and care of the family fell upon her slight shoulders. Her father and older brother were hard workers. Her father worked long hours teaching school, and after school, he worked outside on the farm, and so did her brother. They were loving and kind, but totally out of their element inside when it came to doing "woman's work."

Gwen's early training with Aunt Emma helped, but before long she realized she was in over her head. Besides her father and older brother, Clive, she cared for seven-year-old Janie. There were four rooms upstairs to be dusted, swept, and tidied; four rooms downstairs to be cleaned and polished; and a large basement where she tackled weekly loads of washing and ironing. Then there were planning and preparation of family meals. It didn't take long to exhaust her repertoire of menus.

She rose each morning at dawn to prepare breakfast for the family. She straightened the kitchen, helped her younger sister get off to school, finished her own dressing, and then ran the ten blocks to school, falling breathlessly into her seat just as the bell rang.

Every noon hour she repeated the process in reverse. Home she went at a dead run to get lunch on the table, clear away dishes, and sweep up the crumbs, then run back to afternoon class. Fortunately her teacher understood and was compassionate. On days when she slipped in late, panting harder than usual, ringlets moist at her temples, the teacher didn't scold.

But there was much to do and many things she

simply didn't know how to cope with, no matter how hard she worked or how diligently she tried.

One evening she was more tired and discouraged than usual. The truth is, she was exhausted in mind and body, a little girl overwhelmed with being thrust into the role of a grown-up woman. But in addition, important visitors were due the next day, and preparing company dinner was up to her.

All through supper and afterwards, doing dishes, she tried to think of something appetizing and special. She settled on the main course and vegetables, but the few simple desserts she knew how to make didn't seem to fit the occasion.

Troubled and depressed, she readied herself for bed. As she slipped the flannel nightgown over her head and down around her shoulders, she thought, *What am I going to do? How can I manage alone? I'm not old enough to take Aunt Emma's place!*

That night her stepmother came to her in a dream. Their conversation was as joyous and natural as any they'd had while she was alive. She said, "Gwen, you're puzzled about what to fix for dessert. Have you thought about pumpkin pie?"

Gwen hadn't. Even if she had, she hadn't the foggiest notion of how to go about making it. No problem. Aunt Emma furnished the recipe and gave specific, detailed instructions about how to do it all, step by step. She said, "You've watched me make the crust. You know how to roll it out. As for the filling, remember there are nine ingredients. Count them while you put it together. Be sure you use nine."

Directions were so clear that the following day after Gwen followed those instructions to the letter, the family and guests finished off a hearty meal with pie as delicious, and pie crust as tender, as flaky, as anyone could wish.

There were several dream conversations between the little girl and the stepmother who loved her. During those crucial years when Gwen felt particularly lost and alone, Aunt Emma came to give her comfort. She tutored Gwen on many aspects of her job as premature housekeeper and substitute mother, from washing a pesky stain out of a piece of good clothing to fashioning a cover for a worn piece of furniture they couldn't afford to replace.

We knew Gwen (Sister Williams, by then) when she was older and a homemaker for her own family. She was my closest friend's mother. I remember her as delicate, small in stature, and not able to do some of the hard, physical things other women her age enjoyed. She was by nature loving, with a thirst for knowledge and a willingness to tackle what needed to be done. She was idolized by her three children and by her husband, and I enjoyed visiting in their immaculate, well-run home.

Best of all, I understood that the delicious pumpkin pie I ate at her table—and later at her daughter Clara's table—was prepared from the same recipe given to her as a child by her mother at a time when she knew she could no longer manage alone—and found she didn't have to.

3

Music, America!

Early in 1975, rumors of a planned family theme park comparable to Disneyland, but located in Santa Clara, California, began to rumble their way around musical circles. Most exciting was the fact that the park would highlight live entertainment. It was repeated from first one source and then another that auditions were to be conducted throughout several western states, but nobody knew anything for sure.

One day in October, a talented young Latter-day Saint singing group known as Galena Street East gathered in Sacramento to rehearse for a local show. A stranger came to watch. Wonder of wonders, this man turned out to be the creator of all shows for Marriott enterprises, which was building the park, and miracle of miracles, he singled out four Galena performers for the big show at Great America. Eventually a total of fourteen hundred young people were auditioned. Out of those fourteen hundred, eighteen singer/dancers were hired.

Things happened fast. The performers were taken to Santa Clara, where, out of nothingness, dreams began taking shape. Buildings were constructed and trees transplanted—a fairyland of excitement was being created. One day was spent in orientation to the business Marriott employees were expected to represent. They learned that a multibillion dollar empire had grown from the modest root beer stand opened years earlier by J. Willard Marriott, and it had now expanded to include several parks around the country where families could have fun together. The corporation had long since reached a size where personal supervision of details by the Marriott family was physically impossible. Hundreds of competent employees were needed to make all of the enterprises run smoothly.

The show was strictly professional. It was called *Music, America!* and its featured songs portrayed many aspects of America and her history. The building housing the show seated eighteen hundred persons. A twenty-one piece orchestra had been carefully selected to accompany the on-stage performers. Tailors measured each entertainer from head to toe for custom-fit costumes, even to the measurement of each thumb and finger for individualized gloves. Sets were breathtaking. Opportunities for solos were dangled before dazzled young eyes.

At every turn, these lucky, talented performers were reminded of how special they were. And being especially talented was a necessity. The show was extremely fast paced. Singing and dancing were combined in an almost unprecedented way. Rehearsals were demanding, but possible rewards were exciting, and future opportunities limitless.

Three weeks of rehearsal whirled by, each day more exciting than the one before. Everything went well—until the afternoon the four Latter-day Saint performers returned from lunch and picked up the script for the rock segment. The sacrilegious words leaped out at them. *Prove that Christ is no fool? Invite him to walk across your swimming pool?*

Eighteen young people picked their way tentatively through the arrangement. Three professional choreographers swayed around the gigantic stage, feeling the beat as they went, putting together steps that would eventually evolve into an accompanying dance.

Prove that Christ is divine? Ask him to change the water into wine?

It didn't go well. Four voices faltered. Words stuck in their throats. Steve Seither and Lee Hardy, recently returned missionaries, choked on lyrics that called the Lord a joke, a fraud. Karen Jenson and Renee Digre were equally horrified.

The director stopped the rehearsal. "Come on, you guys. It isn't all *that* hard. What's the problem? Steve, one of your strong points is sight reading. Let's get with it. Once again now, right from the top."

Late that night Steve, deeply troubled, called his parents and explained the situation, preparing them for what almost surely must come to pass. Each of the LDS performers had reached individual commitments during rehearsal, commitments to themselves and to their Heavenly Father, each not knowing at the time how the other three felt. They all concluded that in spite of everything risked, they simply could not continue.

They confronted the director with heavy hearts and explained as gently and as clearly as possible. It wasn't that they were trying to take over his job, or that they wanted to tell him how to run his show. They had really tried, but they couldn't repeat words so offensive to everything they believed in.

The director listened quietly. He asked if they had considered what they were giving up. It wasn't necessary to remind them that they were not indispensable. Specters of 1396 others waiting eagerly to take their places haunted the stage and lurked ominously in the wings. "Let's think this over tonight and talk again tomorrow," he advised.

The four sat up far into the night discussing their options. No matter how the situation was approached, it didn't change. They had no options. They recommitted themselves and each other to leave the show rather than make a mockery of their Savior.

The next morning, rehearsal began as usual. After

two vigorous, exciting hours on new material, they broke for a rest. The director called from the auditorium, "Steve, may I see you a minute, please?"

Steve walked down the steps. The few seconds it took seemed to last a hundred years. The director asked, "Are you still determined not to do 'Super Star'?"

Steve glanced up at the three pale faces on stage. All that they were giving up passed before his eyes. Quietly he answered, "Yes. I can't do it. I'm sorry."

"How about the others? Do they feel the same way?"

Another quick glance toward the stage. "Yes, we do. We all do."

Another silence.

Then, "Well, I've given it a lot of thought since we talked. I don't want to scratch the piece. I'm not trying to make some kind of a statement, but I need it to round out the history of rock in America. How would this work—would you have any objections to going offstage for this bit? I think I've figured out a way to work around you, make it a smaller group. How would you feel about that?"

Steve answered, "We don't have the right to dictate what you put in your show. It's just that we can't take part in anything so foreign to our religious beliefs. If we are completely out of that section, that's all we have a right to ask."

Opening day arrived. The park was packed. Many more than eighteen hundred persons stood waiting in line in front of the theater. The massive doors swung open. People ran to get a seat. The orchestra filed into the orchestra pit to scattered applause. The lights dimmed. Suddenly a tremendous timpani roll filled the hall and bounced off the walls, and a voice echoed through the loudspeaker, "Ladies and gentlemen, Marriott's Great America proudly presents *Music, America!*—showcase of young talent!"

The huge curtains parted, and to the thrilling beat

13

of "When the Saints Go Marching In," the show got underway.

As the fast-paced show continued, it was evident that it was a hit. The atmosphere was wholesome and witty, typical of all that is good in America. There had been wild applause and spontaneous standing ovations throughout.

Then, without warning, the raucous beat of *Jesus Christ, Super Star* pulsed through the air. Fourteen performers in fringed costumes gyrated through four minutes of music and dance as out of place in that setting as if someone had stomped on the American flag. An almost inaudible gasp swept through the audience. At the end of the number four shadowy figures slipped back through the wings, unobtrusively joining in the smash finale.

The show was over. Eighteen hundred people leaped to their feet. The applause was deafening.

As the audience filed out, the cast gathered behind closed curtains to review the performance. The director complimented them on a job well done, mentioned several places in need of a bit of smoothing out, and, almost as an afterthought, said, "Oh, yes. It ran a little long. We need to cut something. Let's skip over 'Super Star' starting with the next show."

* * * * *

"Mother," Steve teased one day two months into performances at Great America, "the only person who enjoys the show more than you do is Gregory Crater, a friend of one of the cast."

Two and a half years elapsed between this chance remark and the following incident.

4

The Crisis Room

As I dressed for my final training session at Suicide Prevention Service one chilly February evening, I felt nervous, jumpy. Would I be able to handle what I was getting into? Why would anyone want to volunteer for a job as crisis counselor on a suicide hot line? That's what friends of all the volunteers want to know. Almost without exception that's their first reaction upon hearing what their buddies do in their spare time.

"How *can* you do something like that?" And then quickly, as if afraid of being misunderstood, "Hey, don't get me wrong. It's great that you do it—somebody has to be there, I guess—but I'm glad it's you and not me!"

What does motivate a person to deliberately step into that tense situation, a spot where each time the phone rings he stands a chance of being the only link between another human being and death?

At first glance, each counselor is so different in lifestyle and personality that no common thread is discernible. The majority are fairly young, between twenty and twenty-nine years of age, although several are older. Many are psychology students in various stages of formal education.

I was searching for a way to become involved in some worthwhile community project. Our prophet strongly encourages stretching our wings beyond the familiar, safe boundaries of Church activity. I wanted to follow his counsel. So when a guest speaker in my college psychology class spoke glowingly of the six weeks of concentrated specialized training available at Suicide Prevention Service, I knew I wanted that training. I wanted to know how to deal with individuals in pain.

"She's gone! She took the baby with her. I can't live without them—I mean it! The gas has been on quite a while now, I want to die, but I'm scared to do it alone. Will you stay on the line and talk to me while I go?"

As I dressed for the class, I wasn't aware of the dramatic struggle already taking place in the Crisis Room at the agency. Strange thoughts and feelings bubbled just under the surface. Training sessions were all behind me now except for this final four-hour stint tonight. We'd learned the myths surrounding what type of person contemplates taking his own life, and we'd practiced composite calls on dummy telephones. We'd listened in on actual calls, with the speaking system turned up, so that all trainees could become familiar with life and death situations before being called upon to handle them on their own.

This particular night one thought kept recurring: How well have I learned? I'm preparing now to save someone who is, perhaps, not yet in need. Who will need me at some point down the road? Will I be able to handle it?

I reached the agency suite fifteen minutes early, the first one to arrive. Some magnetic pull lured me into the Crisis Room, where, as usual, a call was in progress. Cathy spoke in calm, deliberate tones but something in the forward thrust of her shoulders caught my attention.

Most of the calls are intense, serious cries for help, but the majority of callers are not considered to be in immediate, life-threatening danger. If assistance is provided early, most self-destructive behavior may be avoided.

But each ring of the phone carries with it the possibility that distressed callers may have waited too long to reach out. Fairly frequently they have already swallowed a lethal dose of medication, cut their wrists, have a loaded gun at their side, or as in the case with this present caller, turned on the gas with no intention of being talked out of suicide.

"Tell me a little more about your problem. Have you and your wife had serious arguments before this one? And by the way, I mentioned my name is Cathy. Will you tell me yours?"

*"Okay. It's Jim."**

Positive identification of volunteers to callers is contrary to agency regulations. This rule may seem heartless, but it is actually a protection for the caller. The tendency is strong to identify with a voice that provides comfort in a vulnerable moment. It's easy to feel the need to speak to that voice, and only that voice, again. Life or death could well depend on the caller's willingness to accept help from anyone who answers the phone.

"Now, Jim, about your wife. Have you argued before?"

"Not really. Not like this. She said she was going to her mother's for a few days to think things over, but I know for sure she's not coming back."

One common denominator emerges from the varied backgrounds of volunteers. Most have experienced some debilitating personal tragedy. Eric sought out the agency four months after his brother chose suicide as a way out of what he took to be a

---

*Because of agency confidentiality, the name has been changed and identity somewhat obscured.

hopeless trap. A few have terminal illnesses and live day to day with that knowledge. Some, like me, have lost a baby we desperately wanted.

Personal tragedy is like a throbbing toothache; it has to be experienced to be totally understood. No amount of description can allow another person to feel and know the toll suffering extracts until he has been on the receiving end.

"Cathy, I don't know why I called. It's dumb to keep you on the line. If you're busy, I can hang up."

"No, I'm not busy. It's quiet down here tonight. Let's talk a little longer. Tell me more about your baby. I'll bet he's cute."

By this time other trainees have drifted in. The sense of dramatic urgency in the Crisis Room draws them in. No one thinks of moving to the board room for the training session. Cathy's replacement arrives, but there is no move to replace her on the phone. Two staff members are on hand to supervise tonight's wind-up class, and they pace in and out of the room. Occasionally a hastily penciled note of suggestion is placed in front of the tense counselor.

"Cathy, my eyes burn, and I'm sick at my stomach. Maybe it won't take too much longer. I'm beginning to feel awfully funny."

"Jim, I'm not sure your situation is as final as you think. If your wife—what did you say her name was—Sally?—if Sally said she was going away for a few days to think, maybe she'll come back. Is that possible? Maybe you should wait for a day or two to see if it can be worked out. Would you like me to send help?"

"No. It's no use. She'll never come back. (Crying softly, helplessly, now.) I just can't live without her and the baby."

Suddenly a bump, as if the phone has either fallen or been flung aside. Every heart in the Crisis Room leaps in agonizing response.

"Jim, are you still there? Jim? Jim?"
Two or three minutes of heavy silence drag on. *"Cathy? I'm back. I wanted to see my baby's face one more time. I went to get his picture."*

The words are becoming more and more slurred, the voice fainter. If help is going to get there, it's got to be fast.

Suicide Prevention Service is not designed to be a continuing, therapy type of counseling. It is above all a listening ear, assistance at a time of desperation in lives that may not otherwise find the will to survive. Volunteers attempt to identify the immediate life-threatening problem and, when practical or necessary, refer the caller to another community resource for ongoing therapy or assistance.

Many of us carry around preconceived notions about who would attempt suicide. The truth is that this type of desperation knows neither economic, age, sex, nor educational barrier. Frequently callers are well-educated, articulate people. No group can claim immunity to emotional distress that temporarily clouds reasoning.

The sounds of knocking interrupt the slowing pace of conversation. Again the phone is flung aside or dropped from fingers too weak to put it down properly. Hope runs high among us that fate is intervening in the form of a visitor who will be allowed inside. But no, such is not the case.

"Cathy, are you still there? That was my brother-in-law. I saw him through the window and slipped the dead-bolt lock in place. I did it quietly so he wouldn't know I'm here. Now he won't be able to get in.

"I'm so tired, Cathy. Hold on a minute. I'd better lie down, but I think the cord will stretch." More sounds, as if a man-sized weight aimed for the couch but slipped and rolled off onto the non-carpeted floor.

"Jim, I think you mentioned earlier what your father-in-law's name is. It was an interesting name. What was it again?"

"I know what you're trying to do, Cathy, and it won't work. But it doesn't matter if I tell you, because they aren't listed in the phone book. It's Crater—Gregory Crater. He's a nice guy."

Instantly four people search the telephone book under "C." Jim told the truth; Gregory Crater is not listed.

But somewhere in the dim recesses of my memory banks, old information stirs. Gregory Crater. Where have I heard that name before? It wasn't recently. Gregory Crater. There can't be too many Gregory Craters.

I have it! "Mother," I seem to hear, "the only person who comes to the show more than you do is Gregory Crater."

I don't stop to pencil a note—there isn't time. I whisper hurriedly in Cathy's ear that my son knows, or did know, a Gregory Crater. He may be the brother-in-law who knocked at the door earlier. *Hold on, Cathy. Keep Jim talking while I track it down.*

I run to another phone in an adjoining room, with Betty, a staff member, at my heels. I'm sick at heart, because I remember this is one of Steve's school nights. He won't be home. But on the third ring, he answers. Tonight he decided to stay at home to study.

"Steve, don't ask any questions. Can you tell me how to reach Gregory Crater? Do you have his telephone number?"

"No, Mother, I don't have any idea. I haven't ever had to call him. Have you looked in the book?"

Frantically, now—"Steve, think! We've got to reach him. I'm at Suicide Prevention. Think, honey, think!"

Urgency fills Steve's voice too, as he says, "Hang up, mother. I'll call his friend and call you back." The receiver clicks in my ear. As we wait, Betty and I step to the door of the Crisis Room and listen.

"Cathy, do you really believe Sally will talk to me tomorrow or the next day?"

By now it's hard to understand him. Cathy strains to catch each word. There's something about the fragile, shaky voice that strikes an answering chord in all of us. We *want* to save this man. We have invested a portion of our lives into his agony and sincerely care about him.

"I can't promise you she will, but I believe it's worth a try. Death is permanent, Jim. What if you're wrong about her feelings? Tell me where you are."
"I can't think. My head hurts something awful. I can't remember my address. Oh, Cathy, maybe you're right. But I can't remember where I am."
"Yes, you can. I know you can do it. What's the name of your street? When you write a letter, what return address do you put on the corner of the envelope?"
"I can't remember."

The words come more like a sigh than a human voice. The spacing between thoughts is increasingly longer.

The other telephone rings. Steve's elated voice explains that Greg's friend wasn't home, but that his roommate looked through his papers and found his number. Betty rips the number from my hand and dials still a third phone before I have time to thank Steve and hang up. I hear her speaking out as much of the tragedy as agency confidentiality allows. Do they have a daughter named Sally? Does Sally have a husband named Jim? This is a crisis line, and we have information that Jim is in desperate need of help. Speed is urgent. Can they get to him?

Almost before she finishes speaking, there is another knock at the door. This time the knock is heavy, demanding, echoing through the house and resounding from the telephone receiver like a crack of doom. We all remember the deadbolt, securely barring passage to whoever stands on the wrong side of the front door.

"Jim, isn't that someone at the door? Maybe it's your wife, Jim. Maybe Sally has come home with the baby. Get up, Jim. Get up! Go to the door. Let her in!"

The merest breath of response whispers its chilling way across the wires: *"I . . . can't. I . . . can't . . . make . . . it."*

Have we come this close only to lose him now because of a deadbolt? Then we hear footsteps hurrying across the floor, hear one voice call out to another, "Get the resuscitator—quick!," then agonize through the next few moments until the fallen receiver is lifted and a voice says, "This is a fireman. The family called us. We couldn't get in, but a brother-in-law got here with the key to the back door. That was close! We'll rush him to the hospital, but I believe he'll pull through."

Cathy cradled the receiver gently back onto its hook. She slumped in her chair, while twelve trainees and two staff members sagged against the walls or fell limply across a desk. We'd had our first real struggle to keep a fellow human being alive when there was no intelligent reason for his death—and we had won.

Betty said, "Kris, you were meant to be here tonight." And the others agreed.

I agreed, too. I silently thanked Heavenly Father for sending me there on that particular night.

5

The Train That Always Stopped

It was a lovely evening. Springtime breezes stirred gentle fragrances from flowering shrubs. Stars twinkled overhead, and even though she stood on a dark street corner alone, she wasn't afraid.

Eleanor Kristofferson had been fairly sheltered up to that night. She was a senior in high school in Sacramento, California, surrounded by loving family and friends, and now she was on the verge of realizing her heart's greatest desire. Fate seemed to have singled her out for all the best that life has to offer.

She'd auditioned in January with the famous singing coach Maestro Andre de Segurola in Hollywood. He'd spoken encouragingly of her future in the singing world, and had agreed to make a place in his busy studio for her by July. If she saved the money earned by working after school in the J Street Drugstore, she would be ready to begin lessons with him.

She stood on a street corner in an area where stores interweave with the edges of a residential area. The drugstore across the street was dark and deserted now, as was the two-story house behind her, set back among a shadowy grove of walnut trees.

Most nights the delivery boy waited with her, rocking back and forth on his bike while they laughed and talked. Each night their routine was the same: they waited at 24th Street while lights from the streetcar signaled its approach. Just before it reached the Western Pacific station on 19th Street, five blocks away, the streetcar was always halted by a freight train at the crossing. It sat patiently waiting while freight was loaded and unloaded. The process took up to fifteen minutes.

Eleanor didn't mind the wait. She always enjoyed the peaceful quiet of the night, and it was fun talking to Vern.

Tonight was different. Someone urgently needed medicine, and the store owner insisted that Vern start immediately on his rounds. He hesitated before pedaling off. "You'll be okay, won't you, Eleanor?" he asked. Sure she would. Why not? It was only nine o'clock, and at that stage of her life, the thought of anyone wishing her harm was unthinkable.

She didn't realize how vulnerable and young she looked standing on the corner alone. Having gone to work directly from school, she still wore loafers, a sweater, and a pleated skirt. She carried her school-books, one of which she tried to study while waiting, but the stars didn't furnish enough light.

Suddenly she was aware that a car had stopped longer than usual at the stop sign in front of her. The voice of the driver was so soft that at first she wasn't certain he had really spoken. Alarmed, she made out the intense, whispered words: "Come on, get in. I'm not going to hurt you. I'll take you home. Please! I won't hurt you. I just want to talk."

A terror such as she'd never known gripped Eleanor. When there was no response from her, however, the late-model car slipped into gear and glided away. She felt weak with relief.

She glanced down J Street. No sign of the streetcar. For the first time since she'd worked at her job, she felt uneasy and hoped it would come soon.

Then the big blue car returned. It pulled silently to the curb in front of the drugstore on the other side of the street. The door opened, and a tall, slender man stepped out. Perhaps he appeared even taller than he really was to the frightened teenager. He started across the street.

He crossed silently at the crosswalk and approached her slowly without a word, but with each step she grew more terrified. He walked by so closely that his clothes brushed hers as he passed.

But he did pass. Again that overwhelming sense of relief as he kept walking and disappeared in the shadows.

Why hadn't she suspected, after the soldier and his girl came strolling out of the darkness from another direction, that he'd seen them coming and had melted away until they were gone? Why hadn't she taken the precaution of asking the soldier to wait with her? Or to allow her to walk along with them? But her experience in a loving, protective environment hadn't prepared her to expect the worst and deal with it.

The laughing, hand-holding couple continued on their way, and Eleanor was alone again. She was still uneasy, but not panicky. After all, the man from the car obviously hadn't been a serious threat. He'd had business elsewhere. Out of some warped sense of humor he'd tried to scare her, but now he was safely gone.

Three or four minutes elapsed before he reappeared. He hadn't gone at all. He'd blended in with the shadows of the walnut trees in the yard behind her. Now he stood so close that his breath moved locks of her hair with his shrill whisper. "I won't hurt you. Please come with me. I just want to give you a ride. Look at me. Look at me!"

Eleanor stood as still and cold as a statue, looking straight ahead. Some latent instinct warned that her only protection might be to act as if he didn't exist. Any recognition of his presence would be enough to propel him to action.

Without turning her head, she suddenly noticed the light of the streetcar moving far down the road.

Maybe this time it would be a minute early and beat the train. Oh, please God, let the train be late!

But it wasn't. Exactly as on all previous nights, the train thundered across the crossing, cutting off the progress of the streetcar.

She could sense mounting excitement from the man beside her. They both waited for the train to stop. The distance of five blocks was too far for her to expect help from the station. No one would even hear her cries. The rest of the street was deserted. She and this monster who stalked her would end up alone, and she knew that her physical strength was no match for his.

But she did have one advantage. With every ounce of the spiritual strength born and bred in her by her parents, she prayed for deliverance. How long it took, she never knew. It seemed that the wheels of the train clickety-clacked forever. The man interrupted his almost inaudible pleas only periodically to check out the train. He could easily pick her up, hurry across the street, and deposit her in his car, but he would need a little uninterrupted time. A kicking, screaming girl might slow him down. He had to be sure the streetcar was irrevocably trapped. Once the train stopped, they both knew he would make his move.

What else besides the sheer force of her prayers kept that train rolling? Never before in the many months she had worked at the drugstore, nor in the months afterwards, did the train go by without stopping to deliver its freight.

But this time, incredibly, she spied the glimmer of a red lantern waving from the caboose as it cleared the crossing, and the train sped off into the distance.

Now it was time for action. She ran into the middle of the street and raced down the tracks toward the streetcar. It was still blocks away, but its powerful light lit up the tracks. If her pursuer followed her now, he'd have to do it in the glare of the headlight.

He did follow her. She heard his pounding steps

and his words, now more intense than ever. "Turn around and look at me! Look at me!"

She and the streetcar came together in the middle of the block, with the man only a step behind. As the streetcar slid to a stop to let her board, the frustrated man made a last-second grab. Eleanor, who feared he intended to throw her under the wheels, quickly dodged his hands and escaped up the streetcar's steps. Only then did she risk a quick, reflex glance in his direction, and her heart nearly stopped at the impression she had of disarrayed clothing and blurred, white skin gleaming in the moonlight.

Eleanor is convinced to this day that the train must have been scheduled to stop, as always. If not, why not, on this particular night? Later on, only half joking, she liked to imagine the astonishment of the station agents when the train sped past them and disappeared into the night.

Indeed, more things are wrought by prayer than this world dreams of.

6

The Long Night

Alta Reese had barely stepped out into her garage when the waves of panic hit. A police officer's wife learns to live with uncertainty and fear. But nothing in her twenty-six years of marriage to highway patrolman Roland Reese in relatively quiet Logan, Utah, had prepared her for this sudden paralyzing *knowledge* that something was wrong.

It was late afternoon. Final rays of sunset colored the sky outside the garage. Suitcases packed earlier in the day stood by the door of the car, ready for a trip to Salt Lake City, but Alta no longer thought of stowing them in the trunk and driving there. Sick with dread, she hurried back into the kitchen.

"Waves of feelings swept through me, funny sorts of feelings," she says. "It was almost as if I were crying desperately inside, but the tears hadn't reached my eyes."

It had been an exciting day up until that afternoon. It was October 15, Homecoming Day for Utah State University, and especially exciting because Roland, Alta, and their younger daughters, Renee and Ruth Ann, had been joined by their married daughter, Roberta; her husband, Grant Neilsen; and their three small sons. Socializing after the game, dinner, and saying good-bye to Roland before he left for work had eaten up more hours than expected.

But now everything stood poised for departure—except for something inside of Alta that silently screamed out, "Don't go! You'll be needed here at home before the night is through." In what terrible capacity, she had no clue.

Several hours passed uneventfully. The older girls went out for the evening, the children were tucked into bed, and finally, even Alta managed to doze. But her fitful sleep was short-lived. She started up out of bed, the same waves of foreboding alerting her to— what?

Eleven o'clock. She paced the floor, the presentiment of danger increasing with each step.

The shrill ring of the telephone interrupted her pacing, but the message itself wasn't alarming. It was only the police dispatcher looking for her husband. Had Officer Reese stopped at home for a snack?

"I'm not able to rouse him on the car radio—need him to investigate a reported accident on Hyrum Highway," the dispatcher said.

"No, sorry. I haven't seen him. He must have stepped out of his car to write up a ticket."

Alta put the phone back on its hook. At that precise moment, some giant invisible hand seemed to squeeze the breath from her body, and the full impact of the night's premonition struck. Her husband, Roland, was the victim of that accident!

In absolute certainty, she prepared to go to him. She dressed, roused a neighbor to sit with the sleeping children, and was ready, coat on, when a fellow patrolman rang the bell.

It was now close to midnight. Before the officer could bring himself to speak, she said softly, "Just tell me one thing. Is he still alive?"

Frozen in a state of near inner hysteria, she rode the few blocks to the hospital. In panic she climbed the stairs. But as she entered the massive doors, a new stage of foreknowledge pushed back the hysteria and left her strangely calm.

She listened intently to the hurried explanations of Dr. Ezra Cragun, a close friend. Her husband had been chasing a speeder when another driver in his mid-twenties, drunken, girl friend at his side, roared through a stop sign and hit him broadside. The girl was already dead, and the driver's legs were badly injured.

Roland's injuries were still being determined, but even the obvious ones were extensive: broken ribs, his heart pushed to one side and badly damaged. A heart specialist was working with him now. There were compound fractures of the left leg, a broken knee, a shattered right leg, a fracture of the arm, a hole as big as a silver dollar torn from his cheek, his jaw fractured in three places, and a concussion. Even without further examination, it was clear that he could never live through the night.

But the calm assurance borne to Alta at the hospital doors grew stronger. She found herself comforting the distraught doctor, who was frustrated in his desire to prepare her for what must come.

"Alta, you don't understand me. It's not that his chances of living until morning are slim; there simply is no possibility at all."

Alta replied, "Oh, no, Dr. Cragun. Please believe me. Roland is meant to recover. Will you use your priesthood powers and give him a blessing?"

Roberta and Grant returned from the Homecoming dance to find their parents' neighbor sitting in the living room.

"Marilyn, what are you doing here at this hour?"

"They've taken your mother to the hospital!"

Roberta raced back out the door to the waiting car. She didn't even pause as Marilyn's explanation hurtled after her through the crisp night air. "Wait! It's not your mother. It's your father. Your father's been in an accident."

Before Grant pulled to a stop, Roberta flew out of the car, raced up the steps of the hospital, and sped down semidarkened corridors to the emergency section.

Bits and pieces of a tattered patrolman's uniform lay haphazardly on the floor. It had been hastily cut from his pain-wracked body.

She glanced wildly into an adjoining room. There lay her father, one of those unusually healthy people who'd never had so much as a headache that she could recall. Doctors were bending over him, and she saw the raw, ragged bone protruding from his leg.

"No!" she screamed. "This can't be happening—not to Daddy!" Blackness overwhelmed her, and she wilted slowly, unconscious, to the floor.

*   *   *   *   *

It was a strange night. All who came to comfort Alta received comfort from her. She grew progressively more calm and serene after the priesthood administration to her husband, stronger in her conviction that all would be well.

She repeated over and over, "Roberta, Daddy will be all right. Go home, dear. Stay with your babies. I'll need you later to help while Daddy recovers, but I don't need you here now."

The final tabulation of injuries read like a chapter out of an anatomy book. Almost everything breakable in the human body had been smashed, and pneumonia complicated the picture. One week after the accident, Roland suffered a pulmonary embolism. His lungs filled with blood, and he gasped for each breath.

Dr. Daines, the heart specialist, stood beside Alta, a protective arm around her shoulders. His kind, tired eyes filled with tears. "This is the most serious time of all," he said. "Roland could go at any moment."

Alta's firm voice echoed the calm assurance that never once left her during the long ordeal. "No, doctor. My husband will not die. He'll be at next year's Homecoming game. What's more, he'll walk down those steps without a limp."

Roland didn't die. He survived not only that night of bitter crisis, but through the next five weeks of touch and go, vascillating between unconsciousness and semiconsciousness. Flowers filled his room and spilled over into the hall. The overflow brightened every room of the hospital as an anxious community held its breath, waited, and prayed.

One evening Roberta sat alone with her unconscious father. Suddenly, through clenched teeth held shut with wire, he muttered, "How beautiful! Oh, sing it again!" As she moved quickly to his side, he hummed an exquisite melody she had never heard before or since.

At the end of six agonizing weeks, Roland returned to awareness. X rays confirmed that his crushed body was healing as quickly as a healthy twenty-year-old's. Cautiously, the doctors began to express hope.

Dr. Daines was astounded. "To my knowledge no one has ever sustained such traumatic, extensive injuries and lived. It is a remarkable situation."

Roland Reese was released on December 23. He walked out of the hospital supported only by a cane, and returned to a home as bulging with flowers, candy, and gifts as the hospital he left.

And true to his wife's prediction, he not only attended the following year's Homecoming game, but he also walked confidently down the stadium stairs without a limp.

7

Cultural Shock

Several years ago my husband was transferred to Switzerland for eighteen months and we were able to go with him. Switzerland! Just the sound of its name sent little shivers of excitement up and down my spine. Switzerland!—the land of movie star vacations and shooshing down the Matterhorn.

Suitable apartments were in short supply in Zurich. We were lucky. Hans Ringger, president of the LDS stake there, located one perfect for our needs. It was completely furnished down to dishes, bedding, towels—even a hair dryer and typewriter. The only thing we lacked was a television set. All we had to do to set up housekeeping was to carry our suitcases in at the front door.

None of us spoke German. Helpful new friends convinced us we could learn their language more quickly if we watched television. It sounded reasonable. All five of us (my husband, Ed; our premissionary son, Steve; seventeen-year-old Gayle; seven-year-old Ronnie; and me, Kris) piled onto one of Zurich's fabulous trams, rode to a downtown store, and bought a portable TV set.

Part of my husband's work entailed travel around Europe. That day he planned to go directly from the appliance store to the train station to embark on his first business trip to Italy. The salesman spoke very little English, but somehow he communicated that he would take the TV and the four remaining Mackays home in his car and install the set in our apartment. It all went as planned, except that he put the TV in the dining room, which seemed to us an odd location.

On the day we expected Ed home, Gayle and I rearranged some of the furniture. We felt very much at home by this time. We'd learned how to use the washing machine, which literally boiled both water and clothes; we figured out the dishwasher, so different from American models; we'd even managed to escape starvation after visits to the grocery store, thanks to my smattering of high school French. Food was packaged quite differently from anything we could recognize. And directions for everything were written in German, again in Italian, and again in French—never in English.

But we were making it in our foreign surroundings, and perhaps we were lulled into a false sense of our own ability to adjust.

We blithely pulled the plugs out of the dining room wall and moved the TV to a more convenient viewing spot in the living room. I write plugs—plural. There were two electrical cords coming from the set. I didn't consciously notice that until we set it up in the living room.

Electricity in Europe is twice as powerful as that commonly used in the United States—220 volts instead of 110. In Switzerland the wall holes are tiny and round, about the size of lead in a large pencil, protection against some unusual object being inserted.

I assumed both cords had been plugged into the wall because each wall outlet had room for two plugs and they both fit perfectly. We didn't hesitate to plug both of them in. (Much later we figured out that one cord services the rabbit ears and is to be plugged into the set itself, never into the wall socket with its full murderous force of 220 volts.)

That night we welcomed Ed home from Italy with a typical Swiss Wiener schnitzel dinner, and we were still sitting around the table discussing his exciting trip when Gayle wandered over to see what might be on television. We watched idly as she turned on the set and started to adjust the rabbit ears for a clearer picture. She grasped the antennas with both hands.

Suddenly we saw her body jerk and stiffen as if turned to stone and heard her spine-chilling shriek—"Motherrr!"—and then silence. The powerful current glued her to the metal of the rabbit ears. It surged back and forth in one continuous, unbroken circle between her body and the antennas. She was being electrocuted before our horrified eyes.

We leaped from our chairs and dashed in her direction like puppets manipulated by a single string. Even though I knew instinctively that she was beyond hearing, I screamed at her to try to pull loose.

Before we reached her she was unconscious. She fell backwards, and the dead weight of her body hit a marble-top end table. Both crashed heavily to the floor. The force of her fall yanked the plug from the wall, breaking the deadly flow of current, but probably too late.

We converged on what we expected to be the lifeless form of our daughter. I lifted her limp shoulders up into my arms, and she moaned ever so slightly. We picked her up and deposited her in one of the overstuffed chairs that flanked the sofa. She wasn't able to hold up her head or speak, and I saw that her hands were burned a flaming red.

Her father wasted no time. He ran for his consecrated oil, and he and Steve knelt beside her. They put their hands on her reclining head and pleaded with the Lord for her survival. Ronnie and I joined them on our knees.

Gradually she stirred, and we began to hope she might live.

This story has a happy ending. By morning Gayle was almost as good as new. Her inner faith and her righteous, obedient life worked with the priesthood's power even while she was unconscious. Her hands, which were so terribly burned, had returned to normal. A hairline burn across her wrist and a slight stiff-ness of the arms and legs were the only remaining evidence of what by all rights should have ended disastrously—that plus what we suspect will be a per-manent, lifelong aversion to anything electrical!

8

The
Twisted
Tower

It was a hot morning in Orlando, Florida. The sun's rays bounced off the shiny metal of the gigantic communications tower. Loren Williams stood at the tower's base, but of course the shafts offered no shade against the relentless heat of the sun.

Loren glanced longingly at his watch. It was almost noon. The only relief of the day came at lunchtime when he climbed into his rented car, switched on the air conditioner, and basked in its coolness while he listened to news over the radio and ate the sandwich prepared earlier by his motel. The car waited a tantalizing few feet away, but it wasn't quite time.

His gaze wandered slowly up the full height of the tower, one of the few so-called "tall towers" in the world. At fifteen hundred feet high it was a fantastic feat of engineering! Its top pierced the sky at almost twice the altitude an airplane assumes on approach to landing. The tower wasn't very wide at the bottom, only ten feet in triangular cross sections, yet it soared straight up to that incredible quarter-mile height.

The owners made good use of its enormous broadcasting range. Huge antennas for three television channels, several FM stations, and a couple of Highway Patrol translator communication stations were strategically attached to the tower at different levels. And now the UHF educational antenna Loren had helped build in California would be bolted on at the 1260-foot level.

Everything about the operation was mammoth. Nine guy wires, weighing fourteen tons apiece, stretched tautly for half a mile and were anchored securely in concrete blocks the size of a house. Gut straps exerted pulling action at carefully selected spots on the tower to offset twisting of the high tensile steel.

A delicate balance was maintained through regular inspections and quality control of each factor involved —wind load, weight, pulling action of guy wires and gut straps. All were carefully checked and double-checked on a regular basis. Engineers and equipment were housed at the site in outlying buildings erected for that purpose.

Loren watched the crew of experienced climbers swarming over the tower like worker ants, busily making evaluations while their trucks and winches waited below. His own responsibility was to oversee proper installation of the new antenna and to fine tune it on the spot.

He monitored their activities until the crew congregated at the forty-foot level, and the one-man elevator sat temporarily idle. This was the chance he'd waited for. He rechecked his watch. It was finally time for lunch, but at this stage of installation the busy elevator was rarely free. It was the perfect time to look at preparations at 1260 feet. He'd take the elevator up now and still have time for a few minutes in the cool comfort of the car.

As he started briskly toward the tower, a brown station wagon pulled up behind him. The doors opened and three men stepped out. They appeared to be around thirty-five to forty years old. All were pleasant enough, but there was nothing particularly distinctive in their looks or in their bearing.

The driver approached quickly, catching Loren before he reached the elevator. He introduced himself as a land developer doing business in the area. He and his partners just happened to be driving past and had become interested in the operation of the tower. Would Loren mind answering a few questions concerning it? They spoke together briefly, and Loren turned back toward the elevator. Then the stranger asked to look at a transmitter.

Loren hesitated. It was so hot. He thought wistfully of his few allotted minutes in the car. He really should be halfway up the tower by now.

Still, the gentleman's interest in the equipment appeared to be genuine, and there wasn't anything confidential about the transmitter. With a sigh, Loren turned his back on the tower and led the way to one of the outlying buildings and its enormous components of electronic equipment. The man followed.

They were barely inside when the rending, deafening crash began. It came to them as the screaming sound of metals in a long, slow collapse. Their instinct to survive sent them scurrying to huddle down beside heavy iron and steel cabinets. For some reason, Loren automatically counted the seconds. He reached twenty before the grinding agony stopped.

In the sudden, eerie stillness, Loren leaped to his feet and dashed outside. There in a crumpled heap on the ground lay remains of the tower he should have been inspecting, twisted like a mass of molten pretzels.

He remembers his first thought: If a playful giant hand were to hold up 1500 feet of string and suddenly release it, the string, crumpling back and forth upon itself as it dropped straight down, would resemble these twisted and distorted tons of steel.

He rushed back inside the building to the phone to summon outside help, but all lines were dead.

Outside once again, he frantically searched for transportation. One car was completely buried under the wreckage; others were partly covered and obviously too damaged to be of any use.

Then he spotted his own car and grew faint with

shock. Like the crack of a cowhand's whip at roundup time, one of the guy wires—all fourteen tons of it—had slashed through the rooftop, down through the center of the driver's seat, through the car's lower frame, and into the earth below, ripping a gaping hole one foot deep. With sickening clarity he pictured himself sitting at the wheel eating lunch and listening to the news.

But there was no time to think of that now. The boss of the rigging crew called to him, yelling that the boss's own brother was buried in the tangled mass—whether alive or dead, nobody knew. Another worker had tried to jump free and now lay still and white, barely alive with a broken neck. A third man's ankle was badly injured, probably broken. Someone had to go for medical help fast.

Loren remembered the station wagon. Somehow it had escaped damage. At his unspoken plea, he and the three strangers all jumped into the car and they roared off—only to find the one road, the only exit from the site, barricaded. Another gigantic guy wire had broken open on impact and now lay split and expanded to a diameter of five to six feet across the only road from the site. It was impossible to drive over it or around it. Loren knew that the other side of the tower bordered on a lake. There was no possibility of exiting in that direction.

Suddenly he leaped out of the car, shinnied up and over the obstacle, and ran at top speed to the nearest farmhouse half a mile away. The woman of the house had already reached the sheriff on the phone, but relinquished the conversation to the frantic young man at her door. Loren explained to the sheriff that there was no way an ambulance could reach the scene of disaster, so the sheriff immediately dispatched a medical helicopter.

Loren hung up the phone and ran with all the speed his legs could muster back to the fallen guy wire and the station wagon—except that, to his astonishment, the car was no longer there. There was no way a car could have driven away, yet it was gone. Station wagon and men had vanished as completely as if the earth had opened up and swallowed them.

President Richard M. Nixon was in Orlando that day as a guest speaker for an Orlando university. Within minutes he was notified of the accident and called Washington. By late afternoon agents of OSHA (Occupational Safety and Health Administration) arrived to examine the scene.

There was no mystery about what caused the tragic accident. The crew had loosened bolts from one end of a gut strap. They had planned to remove the strap altogether to allow insertion inside the tower of a large copper pipe that would conduct electricity to the new antenna, an operation that had been used three years earlier with total success. But somehow in loosening the strap that day and in shifting their own weight toward bolts at the other end of the strap, the steel began to twist. The delicate balance was upset, and in a matter of twenty seconds, the tower had collapsed.

Loren sifted through the crushed metal and found sections of the 1260-foot level. It was completely demolished. No piece longer than a couple of feet remained intact. If he had taken the elevator up as planned, his body would have been thrown down from that height and would now be as crumpled as the twisted rubble at his feet. Either that or he would have been in the driver's seat of his car, cut in half by the lightning snap of the guy wire.

Without intervention by the three strangers, he would be dead. *Who were they?*

Investigators were vitally interested in the three vanishing witnesses. Lawsuits as enormous as the tower they represented were sure to be filed. Three of the largest insurance companies in the world were involved, along with a hefty portion of their money. These companies and the government itself demanded answers, and if there were three additional eyewitnesses, they meant to find them.

But they never did. Everyone for miles around was questioned and requestioned. Surely men scouting the area for land would have dealt with some of the residents. Exhaustive investigations continued for over three years, and at last, lawsuits were settled out of court for 3.6 million dollars.

No trace of evidence was ever uncovered concerning the men, their identity, why they arrived at that exact hour, where they went, or by what method they left.

9

Bonds
of
Love

There is an endearing tenderness in the love of a mother to a son that transcends all other affections of the heart. (Washington Irving.)

We knew we were in trouble almost from the first moment of pregnancy. Four doctors insisted I wasn't pregnant. They consulted their books and each other and gave me sophisticated tests. All agreed that my condition was caused only by a tumor grown almost instantly to alarming size. They prepared to operate.

I resisted with all my might. After all, I had given birth to two other beautiful children, and there was no mistaking inner signs that a third was now on the way. And I desperately wanted that baby. Maybe desperate is too mild a word to express the love I already felt for this child. I fought all four doctors to keep it.

They reluctantly agreed to compromise. The agreement was that at the end of what I considered to be the sixth week, if even more delicate tests still showed no pregnancy, I would submit to surgery.

And so we waited. Day by day I became more positive that I was right in my diagnosis and they were mistaken.

At last tests confirmed what I knew to be true. The doctors were far from optimistic, however. The tumor was already quite big. There was no possibility of finding out manually what type it was or to what it had attached itself. They warned strenuously against too much hope. With a growth this large this soon, it was impossible to carry the baby full term. Sometime during the middle months they would need to operate to remove the lump.

So we started the long vigil. There's no point in describing the tenseness of those months as we lived them hour by hour while days crept slowly by. Suffice it to say that at five and a half months a series of light X rays showed that the location of the growth made removal impossible without also taking the baby. By this time I walked with crutches.

In spite of continued warnings, all of us held our breath as the magic seventh month approached. We knew that a baby who passed the seventh month has a greater chance to survive. When that time came and slipped by, we were elated.

Then more complications developed, and I was rushed to the hospital. The doctor who planned to deliver slept there nights, with the X rays available at the nurses' station on the floor. The birth probably would be by Caesarean section.

Two weeks went by. It was November 23, 1963. President John F. Kennedy had just been assassinated, although I was one of the few who wasn't aware of it. The rest of the world reeled with shock and grief while I floated in a kind of nether land of pain for which no medication was allowed. If delivery could somehow be accomplished normally, the only hope for that tiny body was to be as strong as possible. That meant no sedation.

I woke at 2:30 A.M. with an intensity of labor I had never before experienced.

Coincidence is a funny thing. The nurse who answered my bell wasn't the competent, understanding woman I'd seen almost every night since entering the hospital. A young, breezy nurse was on duty that night. She took one jaunty look in my direction and assured me I wasn't really in any difficulty we couldn't put up with. She figured she'd let the doctor sleep a little longer. She hated to bother him prematurely.

I was actually almost pleased when hemorrhaging started as she chatted. Now she'd have to do something. She did. She brought in a thick sponge pad to slip beneath me.

The only aggressiveness I could muster was a tone so wispy she had difficulty hearing it. Maybe she didn't hear me clearly. I begged her to call my husband. I reminded her of the danger to the baby. Didn't she understand it must be protected from any avoidable stress? I mentioned the X rays sitting at her desk, ready in case of surgical need. It was no use. She remained cheerful in the face of my distress as if my being pregnant had somehow addled my brain.

The night dragged on, blurred by one continuous, indescribable, pushing pain. By now she didn't bother to answer the bell; she knew what I wanted. Every forty-five minutes she appeared to change the dripping sponge, pat my hand, and reassure me that everything was under control.

Seven o'clock mercifully rolled around at last, and the new shift arrived. Half an hour later an older, gray-haired woman made her rounds. She obviously knew all about the bothersome nuisance in Room 403.

"Well," she said, smiling, "I hear you think you might be in labor. Is that right?" She bent over me, fingers lightly pressed against my taut abdomen. A scowl creased the middle of her forehead, and the smile vanished. She bolted from the room, returning two or three minutes later to say, "Hang on, honey; the doctor's on his way."

The next half hour floated by more or less in a fog. The doctor came, examined me, and cursed under his breath. Orderlies picked me up and gently hurled me—is there such a thing?—onto a gurney, then raced it down the hall. I could feel the clickety-clack of tiles rushing by under the wheels. We careened around corners and bounced off walls. One nurse attempted

45

to inject something into my left arm as we traveled, but the bouncing made it impossible.

We reached the delivery room at 8:02 A.M. By 8:05 our baby had been born, and I heard the thin, wavery cry. I waited for the doctors or nurses to tell me something about the baby. When no one did, I managed to breathe, "What is it?" The doctor grimly muttered, "I don't know. I didn't take time to look." He had forced the tumor to one side, scooped the baby through, handed it quickly to the nurse, and turned all his attention to stopping the bleeding.

The nurse relayed our baby to a waiting pediatrician at the delivery room door, but not before looking to see what we had delivered.

"It's a boy," she said softly.

Half an hour or so later I was moved to a private room. I hardly listened to the doctor. I was so tired and so grateful the ordeal was finally over. He wanted me to be perfectly quiet for a few days. In case anything went wrong, such as more bleeding, he wanted to operate. There was just a chance he would not have to, so he planned to sedate me heavily each night to be sure I had plenty of undisturbed rest.

Meanwhile our son had been placed in an incubator. That's where I saw him for the first time. Later that afternoon I was eased into a wheelchair and taken for my first look at him. He was beautifully formed. The tumor had kept his head elevated, away from pressure, so it was smoothly rounded. His dark hair grew evenly all over like a tiny brown carpet. He lay on one side facing the window through which I peered. His hands were stretched out in front of his face, with one hand slightly cupped and the other resting lightly inside it.

He didn't look scrawny or premature; his little shoulders were, in fact, slightly husky. His coloring was good, and he slept peacefully, dressed only in a miniature doll-sized diaper. I thought again, "It's over. Whatever it cost, we have him."

46

The nurse sedated me heavily that night as the doctor planned. With that much medication, nothing disturbed me, not even the frequent rounds nurses make with their flashlights. My husband and parents stayed with me for as long as the rules allowed.

The second night my husband's visiting time was drawing to a close when the bedside phone rang. It was the doctor, calling with a new problem. Did we remember the disease that had taken President John F. Kennedy's baby a few years before? Ed replied he remembered only vaguely, so the doctor elaborated. It's called hyaline membrane disease, and it often afflicts premature infants. Why, nobody knew, and at that time they weren't sure how to treat it. Sometimes it turns out to be self-limiting, if not too severe. The doctor realized our baby had it when the nurses started to feed him and he went into convulsive breathing. That was earlier in the day. They hadn't mentioned it, hoping the problem would right itself. Now they had tried feeding him again—but the result was more convulsive breathing.

Actually, I was too weak to feel much of anything at the time. I understood the words, but their meaning didn't strike home. We talked quietly for a few minutes more. Then they came with my medication—the same dosage of sleeping medicine as the night before—and Ed soberly left for home.

I had floated in that same heavy oblivion for several hours when all at once I was wide awake. I listened for a noise that might have aroused me. It was very quiet. I felt for some pain that could have reached me through drugged senses, but lying there calmly, I was fairly comfortable.

I looked at my watch. It was 12:55 A.M. I tried to go back to sleep, but my eyes wouldn't stay shut. I pushed the intercom button that connected my room with the nurses' station. It took a minute or two for her to answer, but when she did, she was surprised to find me awake.

I told her I wanted to check on our baby. Did the pause last a fraction of a second too long before her cheerful voice replied, "It's okay, dear, he's still here"?

We had barely rung off when my door opened. A solemn-looking man I'd never seen before walked in, followed by a nurse. The man said slowly, "You were asking about your baby. We hadn't wanted to tell you before morning, but as long as you're awake and wondering, I think we should. I'm Dr. Jensen. I'm so sorry—your baby just died."

Anyone whose ears have never been assaulted by those words cannot imagine what they mean. It had all been for nothing. All those months of hope and suffering, all the agony alone in the hospital bed with no one willing to help, had ended disastrously after all.

What did anything mean in the long run? Why make an effort to live the life you think God wants from you, when there is no protection in times of life and death? Didn't the Lord know or care how much I yearned to bring this precious spirit of His to earth?

But wait a minute! He had come to earth. He had received a beautiful body. His eternal life had been secured. I reminded myself that some spirits are too innocent, too pure to have to be tried.

As comforting as those thoughts were, one thing was beyond argument. Now I would never have a chance to hold him or kiss him or do all the things that build up those bonds of endearing tenderness that weld a mother to her child. Now he would never know how much I loved him, at least not in this life.

It wasn't until several days later that the first stages of unreasoning grief began to subside, more from exhaustion than anything else, and I began to wonder again. What *had* aroused me out of a medicated sleep so deep that nothing could waken me the night before? Was it possible those bonds of love were already so tightly welded that our baby's grown spirit couldn't bear to leave without passing through my room?

I hastily rethought the time sequence. I'd been

awake for a few minutes before checking my watch at 12:55. The doctor said the baby died at 12:50. Had he stood by my bed, perhaps regretting as much as I did all the times we couldn't spend together? Might his lips not have brushed my cheek in temporary fare-well?

I like to think so.

10

Speak the Word Only

As Elder Steven Cameron pedaled his bicycle along the streets of Krefeld, Germany, with his companion, Elder Hunter, his thoughts raced on ahead. They were nearing a hospital where little Marcel Trautmann lay dying. He was only eighteen months old.

As they rode, Elder Cameron thought of that cute, lively little boy and his parents, of what a fine family and how helpful they were to the building of the kingdom. Brother Trautmann was a member of Krefeld's branch presidency. His wife was active in the stake Primary. She was also an accomplished singer and devoted much time to furthering the work through song. Missionaries enjoyed dinners in their home, and their friendly hospitality was extended to all who came inside their door. If ever the elders needed to have someone fellowshipped in an extra special way, they arranged to bring the investigator in contact with this remarkable couple.

One Sunday in August the missionaries set up a family home evening with the Trautmanns and an investigator family. It was arranged for the following Tuesday. Monday afternoon at three o'clock, Elder Cameron dialed the Trautmann home to make sure nothing had changed.

He found Sister Trautmann in tears—her baby was in the hospital. Little Marcel was in a coma with spinal meningitis, which had come on without warning. One minute he had been playing happily, the next he lay unconscious on the living room floor. The doctors held out almost no hope. The meningitis had flared up so suddenly and was so severe that the doctors feared that if he did live, it would be as a vegetable with no mental capacity at all.

Elder Cameron wondered if Marcel had received a blessing. Yes, he had. Her husband and the branch president had administered to him and left it totally in the hands of the Lord. If He really wanted to take the child, they didn't plan to stand in His way. They blessed the baby that if it were meant for him to go, he would die peacefully and without undue pain. They had thanked him for being part of the family for a short time and for bringing joy into so many lives, if only for a little while.

Quite often missionaries have a special link to direct inspiration. The lives they lead are so attuned to spirituality for twenty-four hours a day that at times the veil is thin. Somehow, as he heard the wording of the blessing, Elder Cameron sensed that something more was called for.

Sister Trautmann was in a state of collapse. Elder Cameron asked if he and his companion could ride over and sit with her until her husband returned, and she gratefully accepted his offer.

Now the elders were on their bikes, pedaling the four or five miles to her home. Their path led them directly in front of the hospital where the baby lay unconscious.

As they rode, Elder Cameron kept thinking of Marcel. He felt strongly impressed that it was not in the Lord's plan that Marcel should die. The story of the centurion whose servant was ill came forcefully to his mind. He remembered that the centurion went to the Savior and said, "Lord, my servant lieth at home sick of the palsy." The Lord replied, "I will come and heal him."

51

But the centurion shook his head, not feeling worthy for the Savior to come under his roof. "I am a man under authority. . . . I say to this man, Go, and he goeth. . . . Lord, . . . speak the word only, and my servant shall be healed." (Matthew 8:5-9.)

These thoughts occupied Elder Cameron's total concentration as they reached the street directly in front of the hospital. He stopped. Standing astride his bicycle, he felt impressed to say softly but aloud, "Brother Marcel Trautmann, in the name of Jesus Christ and by the power of the Melchizedek Priesthood which I hold, I command you to be well from this moment on."

They continued their ride out to the Trautmann residence. When they arrived, the mother was still crying. She told them again that doctors held out very little hope for her son's survival.

Very soon her husband came home, and together they all drove to the hospital. Imagine the parents' surprise to see their little boy standing up in his crib, laughing and playing, completely well.

After his miraculous recovery, doctors could find no sign in his spinal column of the bacteria that had caused the meningitis. Marcel went home the next day, well and whole, a lively, happy child once more.

Elder Cameron wasn't surprised. He had envisioned Marcel as a dynamic adult destined to play an important role in a land where strong Saints are badly needed. He knew he came from a dedicated background, and he imagined him a missionary to his own native people, becoming a future leader in the Church in Germany.

How grateful he was that he had responded to that vivid impression.

11

The "Shepard" Who Led Astray

SECRETS OF THE MORMON TEMPLE EXPOSED!

Those words fairly jumped at Elder Rulon Killian. He was a missionary at a time when Mormon standards and ethics were not widely known, and missionary work required all the faith and courage a young man had to give.

This experience doesn't reach us from the pages of a musty journal from another century. It comes from an earlier time, yes; but not as early as one might suppose. A man of our own time was willing, as a youth, to put his life on the line that others may come to know us as we really are.

Brother Killian is now a patriarch in Kaysville, Utah. He has lived a life of devoted service. But there were a couple of days in April, 1924, when he couldn't see this far ahead. In fact, he entertained grave doubts about living long enough to reach his nineteenth birthday.

The eye-catching words were printed on placards and tacked to utility poles throughout the city. They appeared in big, black, bold print under pictures of handsome, silver-haired Mrs. Lula Loveland Shepard, newly arrived in Chattanooga, Tennessee, for a series of lectures on the subject.

Brother Killian was leaving the railroad depot where he'd said good-bye to his former companion and his conference president. This was to be his first experience laboring by himself. With an odd number of elders available, he'd been placed in charge of the Chattanooga Branch. His nineteenth birthday was one week away.

His thoughts went back to Mrs. Shepard. He'd heard about this notorious woman who had made herself wealthy spreading inflammatory lies about Latter-day Saints. She generated publicity wherever she appeared. Newspapers lavishly covered her activities. She lectured two or three times daily: at a ladies' tea at noon, a club in the afternoon, and generally at a church each night. He didn't look forward to encountering her, but curiosity got the best of him, and he resolved to see her in action.

She spoke that night in one of the largest, most fashionable churches in town. The hall was packed, with standing room at a premium, and disappointed people were turned away at the door. He managed to slip in and mingle inconspicuously in a rear corner.

With her on the stand sat many of the city's prominent ministers. One offered a solemn prayer in her behalf. Sacred songs were sung. Then Mrs. Shepard rose to hold her audience spellbound with one fabricated and infamous story after another.

"Missionaries roam all over the world converting innocent women, then ship them to Utah where they are forced into polygamy or mysteriously disappear," she cried in mock horror. "Just recently city employees in Salt Lake City uncovered skeletons of a dozen of these poor souls—victims of the Mormon system. You folks don't realize what goes on among those wicked people."

What a showwoman! She produced copious tears at will and soon had half the audience weeping for the safety of their daughters.

"Now," she continued, "I want you to hear the personal experience of one who was a victim of their treachery."

A thin, emaciated young girl of about nineteen stood up. She spoke tearfully through a megaphone. She'd been converted by Mormon elders on the east coast, she said, shipped to Utah, and forced to marry into polygamy. After the temple ceremony, they demanded she spend her wedding night with one of the Twelve Apostles.

Shocked, she had broken away and run, with several officials in pursuit. She fled through halls, up and down stairways, kicked a window out of the temple, and outran her pursuers. She ran through the streets, climbed the wall that surrounds Salt Lake City, she claimed, dived into the Great Salt Lake, and swam to safety. To anyone who had ever been to Salt Lake City, or who had ever tried to swim in the Great Salt Lake, the story would have been absurd.

After a final muffled sob, the girl induced the vast audience of otherwise intelligent people to swallow her story hook, line, and sinker.

Mrs. Shepard rose again and finally, in a few short sentences, made her motivation crystal clear, but unfortunately, clear only to Elder Killian.

She said, "Few realize what a menace we have facing the safety of our nation. I recently had an audience with President Warren G. Harding. I suggested he send an army to break down the doors of that wicked temple and put an end to this curse, once and for all. He agreed with me. He said, 'Mrs. Shepard, I will appoint you my personal agent to go throughout this country and muster the support I'll need.'

"Now, folks," she persuaded, "that's exactly why I'm here. But it costs money. Lots of money. Ushers will pass among you and accept donations. Please be generous."

It might have been a war bond drive or other national appeal. Patriotic songs were sung while men passed up and down with what appeared to be dishpans. Those pans were filled and spilling over when taken back to the podium.

Mrs. Shepard jumped to her feet again and shouted, "Oh, my dear people, we must act quickly or America is doomed!"

The pans were passed for the second time and filled by normally rational people who had been so cleverly manipulated.

She wasn't through yet. "I have just been informed," she continued shrilly, "that Mormon elders work right here in Chattanooga and hold street meetings each Saturday evening on the corner of Main and Market. Tomorrow is Saturday! How many will go with me to that corner at seven o'clock? Of course, they are all cowards, and they will hear of our coming and won't show up. But who will be with me in case they do?"

Every hand in the room shot up without hesitation —including Elder Killian's. Good sense whispered it wasn't prudent to have his identity questioned at that point.

He didn't get much sleep that night. Almost the last question asked by his conference president at the depot was, "Do you dare continue with street meetings alone?" Elder Killian's confident reply rang out: "They will surely be held, president. Don't worry about that."

A modern civil war raged in his mind all that night and the following day. The left side of him said, "You are a fool if you try to hold a meeting. That mob will tear you to shreds."

The right side responded, "She claims you are a coward. Are you?"

Retorted the left: "Better a live coward than a dead hero."

But the right side held the clincher: "God will protect you."

He climbed on the streetcar and was sorely tempted to climb off again a dozen times before it reached

Main and Market streets. The streetcar rounded the corner, and when he saw the restless, gathering crowd, courage failed him completely and he rode on.

His left side was exultant. "I'm glad you got smart. There have been two elders murdered in Tennessee already [Elders Gibbs and Berry], and you will be the third as sure as you leave this car." And he didn't leave it—not for two more blocks.

Then his right side got the upper hand. It ordered, calmly and positively, "Get out! You are going to hold that street meeting, murder or no murder."

With that side in control and with courage strong, at least for the moment, he jumped off and ran swiftly back to the appropriate corner. He elbowed his way roughly to the center of the crowd, tossed his hat down on the curb with a flourish, threw back his head, and sang one rousing verse of "High on the Mountain Top." The intersection was jammed, and traffic completely stalled. People pressed in around him until he could hardly move. Next he bowed his head for a short, vocal prayer. Then he said loudly, "My friends, I'm glad to be here tonight."

That did it. That was as far as he got. The spell of stunned indecision at his audacity was broken.

Like waves during a hurricane they moved in upon him from all sides, the roar of their outrage swelling as they came. They reached out for him—and a sudden, solid, blinding sheet of rain changed their minds.

What a deluge! It didn't rain individual drops; it came down by bucketfuls and grew worse by the second. This was no ordinary storm. Within seconds the aroused mob was soaked to the skin, as wet as if they had fallen into a river. Women screamed hysterically, men shrieked, and all scampered for open doorways or outstretched awnings.

In the confusion, Elder Killian was forgotten. The storm continued unabated until the streets were empty and he was alone. He boarded a passing street car and returned to his room. He was dazed by the suddenness of it all and by the natural means the Lord had employed to save him from a crowd stirred to mob frenzy by a clever, polished tool of the devil. He knelt and thanked his heavenly Father that his courage had not failed.

Early next morning he received a telegram from Mission President Charles A. Callis. It read, "Elder Killian, I just learned Mrs. Shepard is in Chattanooga, and you are laboring there alone. Get out of town and don't return until that 'infernal female' has left."

He didn't have to be coaxed. He was aboard the next train, speeding gratefully toward safety.

*　　*　　*　　*　　*

When Mrs. Shepard planned a trip to Florida, she wrote the police chief of Jacksonville telling him of her plans to hold meetings in that city. She asked for a personal bodyguard, for, said she, "The Mormons will try to kill me while I am there." The chief responded at once, telling her he would be her special escort, and he was.

After her usual round of infamous meetings, the police chief escorted her to the train. As he bid her good-bye, he said to her, "Mrs. Shepard, it may interest you to know that I am an elder in the Mormon church." (See LeGrand Richards, *Just to Illustrate* [Bookcraft, 1961], p. 276.)

12

A
Battlefield
Commitment

Behind the big walnut desk in his comfortable study, Elder Poecker was deep in thought. As president of the Germany Dusseldorf Mission, he concentrated on the pictures of eager faces mounted opposite him on the wall. How could he help these young missionaries gain a rock-hard faith such as he carried within himself? How does such a testimony grow? What ingredients must be sifted together before being glazed in the refiner's fire? He mused over his own life. Years before, on a bloody battlefield, he'd pledged himself to work for the Lord. This mission calling was only one more phase of his lifetime commitment.

A nostalgic smile touched his lips. It had all started nearly thirty years ago . . .

*   *   *   *   *

When Rudolf K. Poecker was seventeen and first saw the beautiful Elfriede, he knew at the outset there was something different about her. She commanded respect—and much more. Though he was then half a head shorter than she, he wooed her steadily.

While war clouds ominously gathered over Europe, Elfriede taught Rudolf the gospel in their little home town of Fraureuth, Germany. By the time he was drafted into the military, he was well acquainted with gospel principles. He and Elfriede were married while he was on furlough early in the war.

Hitler needed officers. Rudy had a chance to be sent to the Academy of War in Munich, but officers are directly engaged in giving orders to kill. His American missionaries had cautioned, "Brother Rudy, if war comes, remember that all men are brothers. Don't ever allow yourself to enjoy killing."

Hitler also needed medics, and though he'd had no previous medical training, Rudy chose that position. He was put in charge of 350 soldiers.

Six years passed. At war's final gasp Germany found itself in great difficulty on the Polish front, facing Russia. Fighting on the western front had already terminated. On the Thursday before Easter, 1945, a fierce battle raged from early morning until noon. Only seven of his soldiers remained out of the group of 350.

A letter had come telling of the birth of Rudy and Elfriede's first child. How very much he wanted to return to his sweetheart and the son he'd never seen! He knelt down on the battlefield and pleaded with the Lord to spare his life. In the midst of broken and torn bodies, and with all odds against him, he prayed for mercy. "Dear Father," he pledged, "if I am allowed to return home to my wife and little son, I will work for you for the rest of my life."

The German troops retreated to thirty kilometers outside of the capital city of Prague, Czechoslovakia, and were captured. Twenty thousand, perhaps thirty thousand, prisoners were held in the back courtyard of a huge factory.

The prisoners were ordered to post themselves in groups so they could be sent home in appropriate directions. Rudy's seven friends pleaded with him, "Rudy, why don't you come with us? You might be here six months caring for all these wounded men." It was tempting. He was not yet aware of the Lord's guiding hand grooming him for the future. But he elected to stay. This was his place. Earlier he had chosen to work with the wounded, and he wouldn't run out on them now.

Thousands of men were marched off—not to their homes, but to Russia, and forced as slaves into salt and coal mines, while Rudy was kept in camp a total of only four days. But suddenly and unexpectedly, doctors, medics, and wounded were loaded onto a small ship and sent back to Germany and home!

Rudy was barely home when he was called on a mission.

It's easy to make promises to the Lord in times of stress. It's easy to dedicate one's life to righteousness with bullets streaking overhead. Returning home after an absence of six years, Rudy found it hard to leave again, especially when he had no money. Maybe he could have reasoned himself out of it. After all, he had a wife and small child, and he certainly couldn't afford to go on a mission.

But Sister Poecker is a remarkably faithful woman. When the mission president asked if she would support her husband financially and emotionally, she agreed. She not only agreed, she insisted. Her talent for sewing would sustain them.

It was December, two weeks before Christmas. Rudy rode his bicycle home from work. Before he could push the kickstand into place, she raced from the house waving a white envelope. His formal mission call had come.

Later Rudy would speak at firesides and tell the youth, "Many times the Lord puts us to a test to see the willingness of our hearts. When we show obedience, sometimes he doesn't require more of us than we can cheerfully give, after all."

"Brother Poecker," read the letter, "your faithfulness is appreciated. The Lord doesn't require you to go immediately. Stay home over Christmas and report on January 6."

They had eight dollars between them when he left.

Elfriede kept three dollars and insisted he take the other five. The mission home furnished his railroad ticket.

In Leipzig Rudy became ill with rheumatic fever and was unable to walk. He lay helplessly in bed while his companions blessed him and then left for a meeting. Alone and despondent, he felt a peculiar sensation inside his joints, as if they were hardening. Easing himself out of bed, he discovered that he could walk. He hurried to join his astonished companions at the chapel. The Lord obviously had a work for him to do, a work requiring haste, and He didn't intend to be thwarted.

Two months into Rudy's mission, the reason for urgency became clear. The Church officials needed a liaison between themselves and high-ranking Russian officers, and Rudy spoke fluent Russian.

During Hitler's reign of terror Nazi troops had seized records from every church in the country, and used genealogical records to determine who was Jewish. Hitler ordered that the records be hidden underground, mostly in salt mines. The Church of Jesus Christ of Latter-day Saints desperately needed official permission to ferret out and recover those records before that priceless information was lost forever.

Communist government officials are never pleasantly concerned with religious affairs, but to Rudy's surprise, they issued a memorandum granting help from occupation forces in securing trucks and railroad cars. Ironically, this failed to open the first necessary door. Russian officials demanded inventory lists in advance of movement of any records, and of course there were none. Without such lists, they forbade anyone, under threat of death, to enter the secret hiding places.

One day Rudy stood before a particular salt mine for which he'd searched secretly for months. One of the workers agreed to smuggle him below the surface. He dressed Rudy as a miner, and they rode underground in a basket elevator reserved for bringing salt to the surface and were thus shielded from observation by other workers.

Rudy's heart reeled when he stepped into an enormous cavern as big as the Salt Lake Tabernacle and found it filled to overflowing with the records he sought! He made hurried notes of where they had originated and counted them by height of stacks in order to give the Russians an approximate figure. There were records enough to fill three railroad cars.

Rudy touched and gently handled priceless genealogy from the French Huguenots, from prisoners of the French Revolution, from individuals who'd lived in East Prussia, Pomerania, and the Carpathian Mountains—irreplaceable historic documents.

Paper mills around the country were by then busily at work shredding and recycling records of various kinds. Their hungry machines had begun to feed on these genealogical treasures—but just barely. Rudy arrived in time to stop them before any great damage was done. A delay of a few weeks, and they would have been totally destroyed.

Elder Rudy Poecker was released from his mission in May 1948. He had often been hungry. All of Germany was starving in those days. Food was obtained with stamps, and the Russians didn't approve of able-bodied men preaching. They were issued the lowest ration of stamps legally possible.

The little family moved to Halberstadt in the mountains, and Rudy was set apart as branch president. He worked in a meat factory, which was nice because he had access to some occasional meat, but it didn't last. Because he was affiliated with a church, the factory's Communist owners let him go. For a while he unloaded pig iron for a factory and then found work inside a foundry.

A traveling mission president, an American, stayed overnight in their home. Neighbors noticed the American car parked at the curb. People were hungry, and he gave welfare food to some. But because of his visit, secret police searched the apartment. They confiscated the branch papers, membership records and all.

Three days later Rudy was shaving when the doorbell rang. Elfriede appeared in the bathroom door, the blood drained from her face, and he knew something was terribly wrong. She whispered, "Rudy, the police are here to pick you up."

At first he thought they objected to something personal about him, but again it was for church affiliation. He was charged with being a spy, formally accused of espionage for America and of teaching American ideals to German people.

Imprisoned temporarily in the basement of an old mansion, he again sank to his knees to plead with the Lord. "Heavenly Father, when they question me, please put the right words in my mouth, that I may say nothing detrimental to myself, my family, or my church."

It was frightfully dangerous to side with political prisoners. When one was apprehended, it was customary for those on the outside to break all ties with the prisoner and his family. Not so with Mormons. One night Rudy heard an accordion playing "Count Your Many Blessings." Missionaries were walking slowly down the street playing hymns he would be sure to recognize. When Rudy was moved to an established prison, he came to know that strains of "Do What Is Right," usually whistled from the street below, with the hymn's implied message of hope and courage meant that someone wanted contact with him.

His cell was three stories up and behind a high wall, but the sidewalk ran beside the wall in such a way as to make conversation possible. Every Sunday, Saints from the branch drove back and forth and waved to their president to encourage him with their support. A white handkerchief waved from his window let friends know his exact location.

Confinement stretched out for twelve long weeks. One afternoon Rudy's good friend Walter Kindt, a companion from missionary days, came by with welcome news.

"Rudy," he called excitedly, "you will be out soon. The mission president called on the entire mission to fast in your behalf. And we've received word from Salt Lake City that the Twelve presented *your name* before the Lord."

Two weeks later, without explanation, the prison doors opened and Rudy was freed. He didn't stop to ask questions.

That afternoon the Poeckers began their escape from the Russian zone. He and Elfriede cautiously left by different routes. Rudy hitchhiked to East Berlin with individuals who didn't suspect he was just out of political prison. Elfriede went by way of Leipzig as if she were returning to home territory. She packed Rudy's clothes in suitcases and covered them with table linen in a baby cart. As she struggled to boost the heavy cart onto a train between Leipzig and Berlin, a helpful conductor queried, "Madam, what do you have in there—lead?"

The train reached a checkpoint where travelers are carefully searched. Elfriede's heart leaped at sight of the guards. Fortunately their oldest son was intrigued with the officer's gun and showed curiosity. Probably due to this distraction, the police moved on without requiring the usual search, leaving her weak with relief. For Elfriede, it was proof that the Lord was still with them.

The Poeckers were reunited in Berlin's eastern sector, still a very dangerous spot for them. The mission president gave them sanctuary until the American government flew them to West Berlin as part of a group of seventy persons smuggled to safety that month. In 1952 they migrated to Salt Lake City.

Nearly thirty years after Rudy's battlefield commitment to serve the Lord, he found himself back in

Germany as president of the Germany Dusseldorf Mission. He felt he had come full cycle. He had faithfully kept his commitment—was still keeping it. Now he could share with the missionaries under his stewardship the trials and tribulations, the hardships he and Elfriede had suffered through the years—and help them understand that the adversity they were certain to face would develop strength. Tranquility often breeds spiritual cripples, but trials are camouflaged blessings. They are spiritual pushups.

Rudolf K. Poecker has some mighty spiritual muscles.

13

Spiritual Kin

Excitement lay over Western Europe like a tangible presence. The prophet was coming!

For most, this would be their first live contact with a prophet of God. Throughout the German, Dutch, French, Italian, and Spanish-speaking regions of Europe, preparations were underway.

Four hundred German voices practiced in small local areas, then combined to form a chorus to rival the Salt Lake Tabernacle Choir. For months the difficult music of Beethoven's "Hallelujah" filled the air with its impressive *"Welten singen Dank und Ehre, Allelujah dem erhabenen Gottes Sohn,"* as measure after measure brimming over with lilting sixty-fourth notes poured gloriously from the organ.

Native dancers leaped and whirled, and seamstresses sewed typical local costumes, in order to bring their culture to the prophet's eyes.

Munich, Germany, was the site of the third area general conference of The Church of Jesus Christ of Latter-day Saints. The setting was the beautiful Olympic Park built for the 1972 Olympic Games with parking, seating, and other facilities for thousands of participants.

On Friday, August 24, 1973, eager Saints began to converge on the park from all directions. Final rehearsals were scheduled that afternoon. Our daughter, Gayle, one of Zurich's Swiss folk dancers, practiced first, so we arrived early. Broad, sweeping avenues of the park were still relatively free of foot traffic.

We registered and received round green buttons identifying us with the conference. From then on those buttons never left our shoulders. Without them we wouldn't have known that our hotel in town was one big Mormon community for that weekend. We enjoyed nodding to each other at breakfast and later in McDonald's at lunch. That's right—McDonald's!

The theme of the conference inside the Halle or out on the landscaped grounds or around the city seemed to be, "You are not alone." Speakers at the sessions looked out over a sea of excited faces filling the football-stadium-sized hall. Most lived in small towns or villages, and this was their first experience with more than half a dozen brothers and sisters together in one spot. Loving General Authorities stressed how completely they understood the loneliness in being part of a minority in lands where the Church is not dominant and life-styles are so new. The Saints must gather strength at the conference and remember that they are far from alone.

Speakers' words were translated into the various languages and carried instantly to their attentive audience via headphones.

What a glorious weekend! But the most moving moment of all came just after our arrival.

We deposited Gayle in the appropriate basement room of Olympia Halle and set out to wander the historic grounds. We gazed across the highway at the shining white apartment complex where Jewish athletes had been assaulted during the Olympics; we examined the swimming building next to the Halle, looked way up at the tall, graceful Needle, and passed leisurely down a picturesque path rounding a small lake.

"English?" a voice behind us asked. We turned, and there stood a man of perhaps fifty with a woman who appeared to be his mother, in her mid-seventies or so. They were Italian. We were somewhat startled, because the love beaming from their faces was of a kind usually reserved for favorite relatives after a long absence. We felt mildly uncomfortable receiving this type of affection from strangers.

But we smiled warmly in return and said, "Yes, English." They spoke excitedly together in Italian, the one language we are totally lost with. A little German, a very little French, some Spanish we could manage. But Italian? Not one word!

We asked if they spoke English. They looked apologetic and said no. *"Sprechen sie Deutsch?" "Française?" "Español?"* The answers were always no. So there we were, face to smiling face with two people who greeted us with such love that we knew we couldn't let them down. We had to find some way to communicate.

Ed pointed in their direction and said, "Rome?" They shook their heads in unison and answered, "Milan." So far so good. We pointed to ourselves and said, "Zurich." That confused them, and they asked, "No England?" Continuing our one-word sentences, we now shook our heads and said, "California." Then Ed qualified that thought with "Zurich . . . ," raising one finger, and said the Spanish word for year—*año*. Spanish and Italian were, we hoped, somewhat similar.

The man looked thoughtful, nodded, and asked, "Zurich—temple?" Again Ed shook his head. "No. Temple—Bern—Zollikofen." Then he pointed his finger toward the couple again and asked, "You—Zollikofen—temple?"

The man shook his head and then gave us what probably amounted to his whole stock of English words: "Church—nine months." He smiled so broadly as he offered this information that I grabbed his hand and pumped it up and down vigorously, saying excitedly, "Nine months—good! Good! Congratulations!" He really beamed now, so proud and so happy that we understood they were converts of only nine months.

He pointed back to us, and somehow we knew he was asking how long since we had joined the Church. Ed made motions with his hands as if measuring out a foot lengthwise in the air, then more motions of rocking a baby in his arms and said, "Baby." Then he added, "*Madre y padre,*" resorting again to Spanish. They both beamed at us with renewed vigor, if possible, while the older woman kept murmuring over and over, "*Fortunata, fortunata,*" which we both took to mean she considered us very blessed to have had the Church from birth.

After that we shook hands, and with an affectionate farewell we parted. We were thrilled, and I believe they were, too. How completely they grasped the concept of the brotherhood between us. Obviously the thought of not being greeted in return as lovingly as the greeting they extended to us never crossed their minds.

Missionaries had promised them that our common faith makes us all spiritual kin, and in their simple trust, it was literally so.

14

The Black-eyed Spy

What is there about the spy system of the adversary? What tips him off in advance whenever the gospel stands poised for a step forward so he can broodingly observe and sometimes take drastic countermeasures?

Alta and Harold Malan stood at the railing of their ship, depressed. As they steamed closer and closer to Guam, they felt progressively more discouraged. The island seemed so barren, so full of *nothing*. Alta was close to tears. Surely there could be nothing worthwhile for them here to brighten the next two dismal years.

Colonel Harold Malan, three times a bishop, hadn't brought his wife and three small sons there by personal choice. The Air Force orders he carried read "Chief of Dental Services for the Island of Guam."

Brother Malan has a lively sense of humor, but it almost deserted him that day. He gazed out over corrugated metal quonset huts as far as the eye could see and muttered darkly, "I'm tired. I hope nobody tries to give me any extra jobs out here. When I go to church, I'm going to stick a cigar in my jacket pocket and take a rest for the next two years!" He was joking, of course, but that incident reveals the bleakness of their emotions.

Naturally, one of those gray, cheerless quonset

huts was their new home, and when they walked to church, they found that another hut doubled as the chapel.

Poor Harold! So much for his two-year rest! Somehow it doesn't work that way for good Latter-day Saints. During Harold's first morning at priesthood meeting, the group leader had planned to announce his choice for a new first counselor to the assembled brethren. As Brother Malan slipped in the back door, Brother Jorgensen took one look at him, scrapped all previous plans, and called him to the position on the spot. So it didn't take the Malans long to become involved.

Other aspects of their lives brightened considerably before long. The commanding general was one of Dr. Malan's dental patients. In double quick cadence he ordered their housing moved next door to his own beautiful, luxurious quarters overlooking the sea. The rooms were spacious, especially so after quonset huts. The master bedroom windows and a lovely patio faced the cliffline. They had use of an ice-cream-making machine—heaven itself to the three small Malan boys. Life became infinitely more bearable than they originally pictured it from the bow of the ship.

But one thing still bothered Alta. There was a Church youth program of sorts on the island, but no separate program for the young adults. She couldn't rid herself of the compelling notion that they needed something apart from the adults and the youth, a place to express themselves in their own way.

Gradually young adults drifted together on the Malan patio. The setting was perfect for their needs and fostered an atmosphere of unity and warmth. Someone started singing a hymn, and as naturally as night follows day, testimony bearing followed the hymn. The next week these few young people returned, and several brought friends.

Now Alta had a new worry. As the numbers of young adults increased, she worried about annoying the general, who sat more and more often on his own, adjoining patio. One day he accosted her sternly (or so she imagined) and demanded, "What are you people doing over there each week?" She needn't have been nervous. After listening intently to her explanation, his reaction was a brusque, "Why don't more officers do something like this for their young folks?" Soon he found them a real chapel, where the branch's meetings could be conducted in comfort.

But the young people, evolving into a formal Young Adult class, continued to meet with the Malans and continued to grow in numbers. Many of the newcomers were nonmembers. They came because the special something they felt there could be found nowhere else on the island.

One night Alta and her children lay asleep in their beds. Harold was away for the evening. Suddenly Alta awoke with a start, sat bolt upright in bed, and froze. Against the windows leading from the cliff was clearly outlined the form of a strange, frightening man, dressed in a black suit, with a dark complexion and dark curly hair. And his eyes! They also were black and pierced her with a look so evil, so penetrating, she was powerless to move or call out.

At that exact moment, her husband entered. He tiptoed quietly down the hallway toward their bedroom so as not to disturb the family, and as his foot touched the threshold of their room, he stopped abruptly. His breath sucked in sharply with one quick, involuntary gasp. He couldn't see the intruder, but without a word or a sign from his wife, he knew who was there. He said later, "I knew. I *knew*."

Without hesitation, he rebuked the ominous power of evil that hovered there in the room and commanded it, by authority of the priesthood, to depart. To Alta's immense relief, the apparition vanished immediately from her sight.

But the next night it came again. The previous night's scene seemed to have been filmed for instant replay. It was the same time of night—Harold was gone and Alta was asleep. Again there was a sudden awakening to paralyzing terror, and the same dark figure standing in the same spot by the windows. Harold returned, as before, commanded the figure to leave, and he vanished.

The next night brought frightening changes, however. Both parents were at home asleep. Suddenly Sister Malan awoke, but on this night the hideous presence was on her bed with a weight so oppressive engulfing her that she felt certain she would suffocate. Once again she couldn't move or cry out, except for a strangled moan deep in her throat.

Brother Malan has a temper. He has never been noted for his long-suffering while combatting unrighteousness in any disguise. When he woke to that same overwhelming, oppressive spirit filling the room a third time, he began to lose patience. Once more, calling upon the name of his Savior, he rebuked the presence. Alta saw it step from the bed to the floor.

He commanded it for a second time, and it moved to the foot of the bed. Alta was still speechless with fright.

At this point Brother Malan lost his temper completely. He leaped out of bed and pointed his finger in the direction of the emanating evil. Using strict biblical context for his next remarks, and with the voice of an avenging angel, he roared, "Damn you! Get out of here and leave us alone! Get back to hell where you belong!"

This time the figure didn't instantly vanish. It walked out of the bedroom, down the hall, across the patio, and out of their lives.

In the next year and a half, the eight original young men and women in the Young Adult group swelled to a congregation of seventy-five. A goodly portion of the number had never had previous contact with The Church of Jesus Christ of Latter-day Saints. Twelve of these nonmembers were baptized. Who can measure the rippling effects of good works set in motion those many years ago, or the strengthening of young lives in preparation for their own moments of ordeal?

The adversary's spies had been sent out and had returned defeated.

15

Leave the Ninety and Nine

Newly baptized Sister Julie Collins was an influential woman in her area. She lives in a country where the gospel is not yet widely understood, and, like Socrates of old, she buttonholed everyone she met and shared with them her precious new treasures of truth. Fearlessly she spread the word. Once, guiding a civic tour of club women, she stood at the front of the bus, microphone in hand, to bear her testimony. She offered to meet anyone who was interested at lunchtime in the garden to tell of the one true church. Such was her personality and strength of conviction that she was surrounded by those wanting to hear more.

Thus area missionaries were uneasy when she missed church meetings two Sundays in a row. They couldn't call, because she had no telephone. News filtered back that she had a touch of flu. On Saturday morning Elder Frazier and his companion decided to check for themselves.

Outside her apartment building stood Sister Collins's sister, headmistress of a state church girls' school in a nearby town. She paced up and down the sidewalk as if waiting for them, then confronted them with this terrible news: Sister Collins did have the flu, but it was much more serious than that. She was, in reality, a drug addict.

"Mother and I thought your church had helped

her, but now we see it hasn't. We know her well enough to see that she's taking it again."

Stunned, the two young men hurried inside. At the door to her apartment, the mother whispered, "It's okay today. She hasn't taken any this morning."

They stepped inside to find Sister Collins weak and propped up in bed, but her spirits were as healthy as ever. They talked for a while and promised to look in on her again.

The next day, Sunday, a second pair of elders visited. This time her speech was slurred. She was hard to understand. Not only that, a cigarette lay on her nightstand, hidden behind the clock. There was another under her pillow. But she kept repeating weakly, "My testimony is so strong. They can take everything else away from me, but nobody can touch my testimony."

The missionaries were alarmed. They contacted Elder Frazier and said, "You'd better warn Sister Collins plainly that empty words won't get her into heaven."

On Monday morning Elder Frazier and his companion wasted no time getting to her door, but she didn't answer their ring. Increasingly uneasy, they telephoned her mother, asking her to meet them with a key. Instead, the mother asked them to come to her. She thought it was time they talked.

She told a story of surgery some years before, of medication to ease the pain and growing dependency on sleeping pills, of her daughter managing to get them under control, only to slide back during a bad marriage. Before the divorce, she was a true addict.

Not only that, she secretly smoked. And she drank wine with friends when they brought it to the house. The mother, always friendly to the Church, was close to tears. She ended unhappily, "She'll deny she does these things. She lies! She's not worthy to be a member of your church."

If hit by a truck, the elders couldn't have felt more battered. Sister Collins—angelic Sister Collins—lying

to them all this time? Elder Frazier, who had baptized
her only a few weeks before, felt great responsibility
for her welfare. His concern for her now when he
knew she had a problem was no less than before. The
mother loaned the elders her key and promised to
come at half past five that afternoon.

With heavy hearts they went back to the apartment
and rang the doorbell; still she didn't answer. Opening the door, they were hit by an odor so foul it was
like a physical assault. All the shades were pulled and
the usually neat kitchen was spotted with dirty dishes
strewn with dried food, but that couldn't account for
the smell.

They walked down the hall to her bedroom. As
they opened that door, they knew they'd reached the
source of the stench. Vomit lay thick around the room,
on the floor, on the rug, all over the bed.

And lying unconscious on the bed was Sister Collins. Her lips were blue; at first glance they thought
she was dead. Then she moved slightly and groaned.
Elder Frazier pushed a chair over to the bed, took her
hand in his, and said, "It's all right, Sister Collins. It's
Elder Frazier." She groaned again and tried to move,
but couldn't.

They opened windows, got a pan, and, as best they
could, tried to clean up the mess. Her brain was so be-
fuddled that she couldn't make any sense or speak
clearly, but she moaned over and over about the excru-
ciating pain in her head.

Heartsick, the two mature young men remained at
her side the entire day to make sure she didn't take
anything more. Her mother had told them, "One of
my daughters is a nurse. She knows all about this type
of medication. She knows most addicts eventually kill
themselves, but not Julie. Julie is smart. She takes the
strongest doses possible, but never quite enough to be
fatal."

By midafternoon, they risked leaving the apartment to find a phone. They carried all the bottles from

her nightstand with them while they tried to contact someone from the ward. Everyone was either out or couldn't leave work to come. At last they reached the elders quorum president. He could be there in an hour.

They returned to the apartment. By this time, Sister Collins was somewhat more lucid. They read to her out of *A Marvelous Work and a Wonder*, and as her head cleared a little more, they talked of church and last Sunday's sermons. She murmured, "Oh, I miss church so much when I'm not there."

At 4:30, the quorum president arrived with another member. They assisted in giving her a blessing. They touched strongly on repentance and forgiveness, and told her that if she would keep the commandments, she would be well.

In a confused, pitiful tone she pleaded, "Then why aren't I healthy? What's wrong with me? I'm keeping the commandments. What more can I do?" Trustingly, she turned to her special friend. "Why am I not well, Elder Frazier?"

It was so hard! They could see she was drugged. Why did she hide it? Why didn't she come right out and admit the problem and get help?

At 5:30, the two members left. By this time the elders were fatigued to the point of nervous exhaustion, and they hadn't eaten a bite all that long, trying day, but they hung on. Her mother would be there soon to take over.

At 7:30, a young married couple from the ward unexpectedly dropped by. It was necessary to explain the situation to them too, in light of the state of the room, the still-lingering smell, and Sister Collins herself, although it hurt to have anyone see her like this.

The young brother was horrified and cried out in alarm. "Oh, no! A few nights ago she told us she was sick and couldn't get any rest. She thought if she could get one good night's sleep she'd be better. So I went out and bought her twenty sleeping pills!"

There it was. She'd taken them all. That's why she was so sick and almost dead when they found her. Now it made sense—except for the look of total innocence in her eyes.

The heartsick missionaries left for home when the couple volunteered to spell them until her mother arrived.

On Tuesday morning Sister Collins was still asleep when they let themselves in. She'd slept late because the young couple had stayed until past midnight the night before. (Inexplicably, her mother had never arrived.) She was still drugged and groggy, but able to converse on a simple level.

Earlier that morning they'd talked at length to their mission president. They tentatively proposed the only answer that made any sense whatsoever—she might be possessed by a devil. When they looked into her eyes, she looked straight back into theirs innocently, as she expressed her love for the gospel. How could anyone lie so convincingly except through possession?

The president counseled them, "It's possible, of course. Go back again and see what you think today. You brethren hold the same priesthood I do. You go back, determine the problem, and do whatever is necessary."

On the way back another thought began to surface. Could it be that a prescription by her doctor for the flu worked antagonistically with another medication? Could she be taking it innocently?

They challenged Sister Collins not to take any medicine at all, to rely solely on the power of the blessing. She appeared willing to try anything they suggested. They hoped that if she promised faithfully not to take anything, she might discard the damaging pills. So she gave them everything—antibiotics, cough syrup and all—everything except the real thing.

They persisted. Did she keep anything else for

guests perhaps, like wine or cigarettes or something stronger? No, she didn't.

Later that day they slipped out to the garbage and salvaged the bottles. If she wouldn't give up the pills, it was senseless to waste the doctor-ordered prescriptions, but they stored them in a kitchen cabinet, out of sight. They too would put their faith in the strength of the blessing.

On Wednesday morning she met the elders at the door, looking much better. Some of the sparkle was back in her eyes, and her thinking processes were clearer. They put it to her straight. They wanted to phrase their concerns in such a way that she wouldn't think they were angry with her, but they knew Satan can work through people and he can lie through their lips.

They said, "Sister Collins, we know you're a good person. We realize you want everyone to know what a strong testimony you have. But sometimes Satan tempts us to do things we don't want to do. When we slip, we're afraid someone will find out and think the worst of us. Sometimes we try to hide what we've done."

A curious look passed over her face and she asked, "What do you mean?"

They went on. They had reason to believe she had a problem with the Word of Wisdom. They mentioned the cigarettes they'd found behind the clock and under her pillow, and the coffee grounds in the wastebasket. She was shocked. "How did they get there?"

"Sister Collins, your mother and sister tell us you use these things."

Now she was really shocked. "Why would they say something like that?" she cried.

"Sister Collins, have you ever taken sleeping pills?"

"No, I haven't. I don't understand what you're asking!"

"What about the pills your friend bought?"

"Yes, I wasn't able to sleep, and he got me something to help. After he left, I thought about what you taught me before I joined the church. You said drugs are not good for the body, and I flushed them down the toilet."

She had a logical explanation for everything. Her answers did explain each item, but the difficulty was, nobody was ever there to witness her actions. And, of course, the most damning evidence of all was when they had walked in and found her almost dead.

The elders were frantic with concern for her. They didn't know where to turn. They remembered her mother saying, "She lies!" They thought of the mission president saying that Satan lies better than we possibly can. They had pursued and discarded every angle they could think of except the final possibility that she was possessed. When they spoke of it, she started to cry. They emphasized that it was only a possibility; they weren't sure. Would she like a blessing just in case?

They couldn't bear to let her hear the words, so their prayer was offered in English, not in her native tongue. They commanded the devil, if actually there, to leave, and they promised her protection from evil influence as long as she kept the commandments.

On Thursday morning they were back. She looked almost like the strong, self-reliant woman they'd thought they knew so well.

She invited them in and said, "Yesterday was the saddest day of my life. After you left, I started to do my dishes. Confused thoughts about three days I can't account for filled my mind, and I thought about what my mother and sister had said about me. I cried so hard I almost didn't need to pour out water to wash the dishes; my tears were enough to do the job."

As she had tried vainly to sort out the strangeness of the past few days, a neighbor knocked on the door.

Her sister, the nurse, was on the neighbor's telephone, checking to see how Julie was. Julie went to the phone, and as they talked, suspicions began to fall into place. She remembered feeling sick directly after her sister left her on Sunday morning, just prior to the visit of the second pair of missionaries.

Suddenly she knew. She asked angrily, "What did you give me?"

Silence on the other end. More fiercely, Sister Collins demanded, "What did you give me?"

The nurse broke down and told how much her family was worried about Sister Collins. "You depended so completely on those young, inexperienced missionaries and their new church. You didn't even want a priest—one who has studied for years—when you were sick.

"We talked it over, and I gave you a strong sedative. I put it into your cough medicine. We thought that if the missionaries believed you were an addict, they wouldn't want anything more to do with you, and you would return to our church.

They had formulated a convincing plan to present so that the missionaries would be prepared to believe the worst, and then had set it up for them to find her unconscious with a cigarette under her head. They admitted it all when confronted. They gave her as strong a dose as they dared so that when the elders walked in, they would be sickened and would desert her; then, in her weakened, lonely, disillusioned position, she would ask for a priest. They counted on the missionaries giving up on her and never coming back.

What her family didn't take into account was that they were not dealing with an ordinary church. Sister Collins belongs to the church of the Lord. The young men loved her. They thought she had a problem, and they persisted in trying to help.

After all, didn't their Shepherd say to leave the ninety and nine and go after the one who is lost?

16

A Welcome Voice

As Ed strode through the enormous Japan Steel Works factory toward the adjoining guest house, he felt the first twinge of unsettling pain. It struck on the right side of his back, just below the ribs. It wasn't too bad at the moment, but there was no doubt what it was.

A tendency to have kidney stones runs in the Mackay family. As Ed was growing up, it wasn't unusual to see his father carried home from work unconscious from an attack; and as they grew older, the seven Mackay brothers fell heir to this unwelcome legacy. The pain involved is one of the most severe to which the body can be subjected.

Ed was lucky. He'd had only one attack years ago at home with his family doctor close by. It had been rough, but he'd had the support of family and friends. Here in Muroran, Japan, he was half a world apart from that support, and as far as he knew, only one other man in the entire area even spoke English, his company-appointed interpreter.

Ed quickly evaluated his position as the pain increased. If someone were to instigate a contest for "Most Remote Spot on Earth," Muroran would be high on the list of contenders. The city itself is located a mile from the factory on the island of Hokkaido, the northernmost island of the chain. In winter bone-chilling winds whip across the narrow Sea of Japan from the icy wastelands of Siberia. This was July. At least the weather was on his side.

The resident population of the area is made up entirely of Japanese workers. There are no western-type hotels, no recreation that Ed could detect during his lonely strolls through town, no tourist attractions of any kind. In a country famous for its exquisite gardens with delicate curved bridges poised over sparkling pools of water, Muroran is noted strictly for its no-nonsense contribution to the Japanese economy.

There certainly were plenty of people in Muroran —friendly, polite, gentle people, smiling cordially and bowing, as hospitable as possible to a stranger whose language and customs are so far removed from their own. But for a lone American, there was almost no common meeting ground for socialized communication.

It wasn't just the language. Japanese food seemed so foreign to Ed's uninitiated tongue, especially the ubiquitous morsels of raw fish tucked into the most unlikely dishes, even their versions of potato salad and spaghetti. Even the size of the workers, so small compared to his own six feet four inches, served to set him apart. All the facets of the culture, so fascinating to him just a short time before, now added to his sense of isolation when he suspected he might soon need to ask for help.

He made it back to his tiny room and stretched out across the bed. One hand clutched his aching back while beads of perspiration formed on his forehead. What should he do?

His eyes took in the telephone next to his head. Whom could he call? He'd already checked out the phone book for signs of a Mormon church or mission home. He really didn't expect to find one, and besides, the book was written in Kanji script and was completely illegible to him.

By now the pain was too severe to be ignored. Apparently this would be a serious attack. He'd have to try something.

He picked up the receiver. With little hope of being understood, he explained he needed a doctor fast. Something in his tone must have alerted the receptionist that he was in trouble, and ten minutes later his interpreter knocked at the door to find out why. The company hospital wasn't far away. Mr. Ohtsubo called a taxi and took him there.

For the next torturous hour and a half, a doctor methodically gathered Ed's medical history. He asked questions in Japanese, which were translated into English by Mr. Ohtsubo. Ed answered them through clenched teeth while he dripped with perspiration from the effort. The English answers were then converted to Japanese and relayed back to the waiting physician. It was a long, laborious process.

He lay face down on a small padded bench with feet and legs dangling off the end, in a sterile, austere room.

The doctor finished his lengthy questioning, thumped Ed's back up and down several times, and finally came to his considered conclusion. This time he spoke directly to his patient, the first indication that he understood any English at all.

He enunciated slowly with hesitation between each syllable: "Mr. . . Mac-kay, . . . it . . . is . . . my . . . o-pin-i-on . . . you . . . have . . . kid-ney . . . stones." Ed groaned under his breath. He was definitely in agreement about that!

A powerful painkiller was administered, followed by X rays showing three stones. Now it was a matter of waiting. The hospital was small, so the doctor sent him home with instructions to return the next morning. If the stones hadn't passed, the doctor would consider removing them by surgery at that time.

Ed had never felt more helpless and alone. We grow accustomed to calling on spiritual brothers and sisters in times of crisis. When the gospel is rapidly spreading worldwide, it seems unthinkable to find oneself in a place where that support is not available. But that's the situation Ed found himself in.

Mr. Ohtsubo escorted him back to his room and promised to look in on him a couple of hours later. Ed's head grew heavy as the shot took effect. He peeled the drenched clothing off his dripping body, wringing wet from head to toe. He showered briefly, then fell asleep.

The ringing of the phone woke him an hour later. The shot was wearing off, and the pain was returning, stronger than ever. He debated with himself whether or not to make the effort to answer the phone. The call must be a mistake. Even if he answered, how could he communicate with the person on the other end? But the ring was insistent, and he finally moved his hand to the receiver and managed a hoarse, "Hello?"

"Brother Mackay?" came the cheery reply. "This is Elder Hutchison. My companion and I were tracting the other day and heard rumors of a tall American staying at the steel works guest house who never drinks tea. We wondered if you might be LDS. We're in the lobby. Would you mind if we come up for a minute?"

Mind? Ed gripped the phone tightly. The room swirled. He was dizzy with pain, remnants of medication, and relief, but now he would be all right. Even in this remote spot he wasn't really alone, and he knew from experience what can be accomplished between two priesthood holders and one who believes.

"Elder," he sighed, "you'll never know how glad I am to hear your voice! By all means, come up. And Elder Hutchison—HURRY!"

17

Fringe Benefits

Max Lieber walked into the mission president's office in Zurich, Switzerland. He lives in Winterthur, an old, tree-lined town roughly twenty-five kilometers northeast of Zurich, where he works as a chemical engineer dealing with plastics, traveling on occasion to fairs or exhibitions in other European countries. He likes his job, and finds it exciting and challenging to work with man-made materials unknown until one hundred or fifty or even twenty years ago. But mainly he is a remarkable human being and a dedicated member of the LDS church.

Max's purpose on this particular day was to offer his services to anyone who might need him. He explained to the president that an exhibition called him behind the Iron Curtain. He wondered if there might be something he could do for any of the members there.

The president looked up thoughtfully. "Well," he said, "I'm not too up-to-date on happenings in that part of the world. Another mission is our direct contact with those people now. They live closer and find it easier to cross over the border than we do. But as long as you'll be there anyway, why don't you check with a certain brother and, if you can manage it, give him two or three of our books. But be careful. It's not wise to be open or to speak of these things to anyone along the way!"

He handed Max the address of a man who acted as branch president, trying to do what he could to hold the people together under trying circumstances. Strangely enough, the branch president's house lay directly across the street from the fair.

Once he arrived, Max walked across the street to the man's door. He rang the bell, and shortly a man came out.

"Are you Mr.____?"

The man answered pleasantly, "Yes, I am."

"Then you must be Brother ____, as well."*

A shadow fell across the man's face. He quickly lifted his forefinger to his lips in a gesture of silence. His nervous eyes scanned up and down the street before he took Max's arm and led him into the house, finger still motioning for silence. As they walked, his mouth moved without sound and formed these words: "Please! Don't say anything more."

Before another word passed between them, he hurried to the telephone. Carefully he lifted the phone onto an enormous cushion on a convenient spot on the floor and packed pillows over and around it until he was satisfied that it was safely muffled. "Now we can talk," he sighed.

Still softly, he questioned Max about his errand in the city. They spoke of Max's business interests there and of his love for the gospel that led him to risk contact with members. Max took out the books from his briefcase and placed them in the other man's hands. They were his to use as he saw fit, or if he dare not, to destroy.

The tension on his new friend's face eased and he said, "Yes, of course we can use them," and he seemed pleased with the gift, but wasted no time tucking them out of sight.

Now it was his turn. He recounted stories of his little flock there, of difficult hours, and of being closely

---

*Because of possible consequences to members still in Iron Curtain countries, names of people and places have been omitted.

watched by the police at all times in all their activities. Their meetings, such as they were, were held in secret in private homes, not openly as he understood was allowed in some Communist countries.

Baptisms were no longer permitted, but behind the Iron Curtain members and nonmembers alike learn to cope with life as it is forced upon them. Church members had succeeded in building a small swimming pool in his garden. The police were informed that its purpose was to provide summer fun for the children. Of course, it was located in such a way as to make an occasional baptism possible once again. Even in those frightful surroundings the work, more important to them than food or drink, went slowly on.

As a father, his chief concern was for the welfare of his five children. "It's so difficult to raise children strong in our belief when the state does all it can to separate them from the family. The state influences them from an unbelievably early age—it's all part of the Communist system. Am I going to be able to combat that sufficiently with what little I can do here?"

Max gripped his hand in parting and shook his head in wordless sympathy. He didn't know what else to do at the moment, but he promised to come again.

His second trip came some months later, following a youth conference held in Frankfurt where he had been approached by a girl he didn't know. Eagerly she said, "You're Brother Lieber, are you not? I've heard you sometimes visit my home country. Would you check on my parents if you go again?" Max willingly agreed.

He stopped first at the home he'd visited earlier. The good brother hurried him inside as before, but appeared greatly agitated.

"I knew you were coming," he said in hushed tones. "What inspired you to come to me first? They have been watching that other home and are waiting for your arrival. You would have been picked up by the police the moment your finger touched the bell.

That girl foolishly wrote her parents that *Brother* Lieber was coming."

A shiver passed through Max, as if a cold wind had suddenly passed through the room. He had experienced interrogations behind the Iron Curtain. Usually they amounted to no more than that—interrogations—but the officials kept the unfortunate person under suspicion for up to forty-eight hours, questioning him closely, deeply, and it wasn't pleasant. He was grateful for whatever inspiration had led him away from the trap.

This was almost certain to be his last trip to the city. Already he'd filed an application to change jobs to one that allowed travel in the United States. A rather long and detailed discussion followed, after which the brother thought for a moment, then brought out a packet of money.

To the eyes of someone from the free world, the amount was small. The brother had saved it out of his personal earnings, and the amount constituted roughly one month's pay. It was earmarked for use in case any family member managed to travel abroad. They longed to be able to visit the Swiss Temple; the present political situation seemed to allow some hope for that possibility.

Would Brother Lieber risk taking the money out of the country? In the event no one ever got the chance to travel, the money should be turned over to the Church and considered as part of the family's tithing contribution.

He realized he asked a lot. The amount was small, but it represented many months of scrimping and restraint. It was his total life's savings, given over into the hands of a comparative stranger. He had no idea when he would be able to claim it, but it would be comforting to know it was there.

For Max's part, this was indeed no small request. The penalty for smuggling money out of Communist countries is severe. In Russia, for example, the death sentence is not uncommon. Certainly several years in jail would be the least to expect even for an amount of this size. But he had offered his help in good faith, and now he was in a position to give it, if he dared.

He took the money and then spent long hours considering different aspects of his luggage. What spot would be most safe from the prying fingers of border guards and allow the hidden money, and Max himself, to pass by safely?

* * * * *

Two years later Max was hard at work at the Boeing plant in Seattle, Washington. Late one night the telephone roused him from a deep sleep. The clock on his nightstand showed 1:30 A.M. When he drowsily answered the phone, an operator announced a long-distance, collect call from Munich, Germany. Would he accept the charges?

Max was puzzled and blinked the sleep from his brain. Whom did he know in Munich?

Much to his amazement and delight, it was the friend he'd met behind the Iron Curtain. He had finally been able to gather his family and flee his country. At last his children could be reared in freedom and according to the gospel standards. They'd already been accepted by the Canadian government and would be allowed to immigrate to a new life. But they had come away destitute. Did Max still have that money?

Of course Max did. And happily it was more than the brother expected. Max had exchanged it for the official rate through his company, not for one quarter of its value through the black market exchange. "Your money will be delivered to you as soon as it can get there!" he promised.

Now the love that had begun in secret between the Lieber family and their good friends could grow openly. Before long, Max and his wife, Suoma, drove to Canada to pay them a visit. The Liebers found the family living frugally, but obviously rejoicing in their new life of freedom.

There had been only two previous meetings between them, yet one man had relinquished his entire life's savings to the other, never doubting the money would be available when, or if, he came to claim it.

One of the great fringe benefits of our Church membership is the bond that exists between us as brothers and sisters in the same eternal family.

18

A
Miniature
Suoma

The first furniture Max and Suoma Lieber bought was rugged and durable, made to resist wear and tear from the house full of children they expected before long. They childproofed their home, filled it with love, and confidently waited.

But the years slipped away, and no children came to them.

At first they weren't overly concerned; Sue's patriarchal blessing clearly promises all the blessings of motherhood. One year followed another, however, and still their furniture stood unblemished by any scuffings of tiny feet. Once or twice their thoughts touched fleetingly on the subject of adoption, but they had decided to wait just a little longer, still hoping Suoma would be able to bear a child.

The time came when their longing for children could no longer be denied. They were living in Winterthur, Switzerland, but were sent to the official adoption office in Zurich. Voluminous stacks of papers were carefully prepared, and all seemed to go well until they came to the question of religion. Once they had written down their church affiliation, the doors of cooperation closed.

"You will never get a baby," said the worker coldly. "Babies are placed in homes reflecting the natural parents' faith, and I wouldn't sit around waiting for a

Mormon baby if I were you. There's always a chance, of course, that a Mormon child might become available, but don't count on it. I've seldom known it to happen."

Max and Suoma were disappointed beyond words to describe. They had felt anguish through the lonely years, but aways had confidence that when all else failed, ultimately they could turn to adoption. Now even that possibility was being denied them, and there was nowhere else to turn.

A few nights later Suoma dreamed a dream as real to her as any experience of her life. She dreamed she sat in her apartment watching two women near her door. One lovingly held a baby in her arms and announced her intention of giving it to the Liebers. The other woman grasped her shoulders harshly. "No!" she said. "They can't have her. They are Mormons. If they change their faith we can help them. Until they do, there will be no babies for them."

But the first woman shrugged off the cruel grasp, continued resolutely down the corridor, and stopped outside the door. "This is the Lieber baby," she answered firmly, "and I intend to see that they have her."

She opened the door, stepped across to Suoma, and gently laid the tiny bundle in her outstretched arms. Sue drank in every feature of the little face as if she were starving, and the sight of the baby nourished the very center of her soul. The baby, blonde and fair, with light blue eyes, was smiling back at her.

The dream slowly faded, and Sue's first waking reaction was confusion. She looked at her empty arms. Where was her baby? Just a second ago she had held her, and now she was lost. She searched through the bed covers. The baby was truly, undeniably gone, and all the pent-up longing and frustration issued forth in great, gasping sobs of hopelessness.

She was careful not to speak of this dream to many people; it hurt too much. But to her husband she cried out over and over again, "Why did I have to be troubled with that sight when it was only a dream and will never, never come true?"

Fortunately time eases all pain, and the human mind seems to be able to adjust to situations it cannot change. The Liebers continued their busy, useful, even enjoyable—though childless—lives. It's true that once or twice their thoughts returned to the suggestion in the dream. Would it be so terrible to briefly renounce their faith to accomplish their heart's desire? They had so much love to give, and surely there were little spirits who needed that love. Wouldn't the Lord understand and forgive if they pretended for a time, being careful all the while to keep the truth deep within their hearts?

But these thoughts lasted only a moment—*ein Augenblick* in their descriptive German tongue, the blink of an eye—and were never seriously entertained. For better or for worse, their feet were firmly planted on the road of truth, and if they were destined to travel that road alone, just the two of them, so be it.

Two more years passed. They moved back to their original home, to the house where family life had begun so hopefully for them fifteen years before. This was their permanent home now, and they set about to make it comfortable. The sturdy furniture was discarded, and in its place they ordered new pieces. Utility and ability to withstand abuse were no longer factors. For couch and matching chair fabric they chose a stylish brocade. They picked a coffee table of gleaming, polished wood. A modern floor lamp completed the living room, and they were pleased with the results.

Soon thereafter Suoma sat in the foyer of the stake center in Zurich, waiting for stake conference to begin. To pass the time, she played with a friend's little girl. She glanced up as a sister she knew only slightly approached her. The sister asked a surprising question.

"Suoma, have you ever thought of having a baby of

your own? Would you ever consider adoption?" The sister went on to explain that she worked for an agency in a nearby town, and she picked up newborn infants from hospitals and carried them to a place of waiting while parents and children were sorted out and matched together. Was there any possibility Sue would be interested?

Sue listened in stunned silence. She felt glimmers of returning hope that she had fought so long to conquer. Quickly she told her long, frustrating story. She spoke of the law that prohibited adoptive parents from claiming any but children of their own religious affiliation.

The sister frowned. That simply wasn't true. There was no such law. Granted, that was custom and it was nearly always followed, but it wasn't ironclad law. Perhaps it would be wise to recheck, and in the meantime, she would contact her boss.

The next morning Max and Sue hurried eagerly to the original agency in Zurich, where their papers were still on file after eight years, but inactive. The same woman greeted them coolly. No, she admitted, the practice wasn't written into law, but she was no more encouraging this time than last. They urgently pressed her, and finally, reluctantly, she agreed to send their papers to the official in charge of their friend's agency. But along with the papers, she enclosed a note.

"I was very impressed with this couple eight years ago," she wrote. "They seemed sincere and responsible, and I felt they would be excellent parents—until I learned they were Mormons. I don't know if you realize it, but Mormons are different from other people. They are a close knit group. They don't mingle with anyone else in the community. Their lives are stunted by the small circle in which they move, and in my opinion, it would be detrimental to a baby to be delivered into such a restricted atmosphere."

But the new official knew better than that. His own assistant was a Latter-day Saint, and when she was

97

able to reassure him about the life-style of the Liebers —that Max was president of a weekly accordion club and the only Mormon of that group, that he was a respected worker in his field, that Sue took active part in her town's Finnish club and otherwise participated in community affairs—he was satisfied. He reached for the phone and made an appointment to visit with them personally.

A week after his visit, the phone rang again in the Lieber home. Their baby was waiting.

The baby was blonde and fair, with light blue eyes, and she smiled back into Suoma's own smiling face.

What set this miracle in motion? It wasn't until little Annikka lay safely in her mother's arms that they heard the true story.

One morning the sister who had approached Suoma in the stake center had gone on her usual errand. When she looked down into the crib, a strong feeling of recognition came to her. "That's Suoma Lieber's baby," she gasped. "I know it is. She looks exactly like her, and I intend to see that the Liebers have her. How can I make Sue understand that this baby is really hers?"

The following day was stake conference. She'd never known the Liebers to miss a meeting, and she made it a point to be there.

*   *   *   *   *

We returned to Switzerland during the summer of 1980 and visited with Max and Sue in their home, the home where we first met. It seemed so natural to see them there again, in familiar surroundings, but this time as we climbed the stairs, we dodged around a stroller lodged on the landing. We stepped over a low gate that barred the top of the stairs. A bright orange teddy bear sat casually on the beautiful brocade couch, not matching the color scheme too well, but somehow it seemed perfectly at home there.

Then a door burst open, and in bounced a miniature twenty-month-old Suoma. It wasn't that she looked like Sue, she *was* Sue, shrunken by some magic to this tiny size.

Pictures hadn't prepared us for the shock of seeing her. The coloring of her hair, her skin and eyes, the bone structure of her face, eyes with that same Finnish upward slant at the corners—no one would dare deny this was Suoma's child. The strange coincidence was that out of all the millions of mothers and children on earth, they finally came together.

Coincidence? Not really.

"And moreover, I would desire that ye should consider on the blessed and happy state of those that keep the commandments of God. For behold, they are blessed in all things both temporal and spiritual; . . . if they hold out faithful to the end. . . . O remember, remember that these things are true; for the Lord hath spoken it." (Mosiah 2:41.)